veggies

okra garlic

kale

onion

celery

corn

give

ck

it's good Shit

chopped

street food

eat like you

tacos

fresh

fruit

VI2039

THUG

KITCHEN

*eat like you give a f*ck*

Rodale books may be purchased for business or promotional use or for special sales. For information, please write to: Special Markets Department, Rodale Inc., 733 Third Avenue, New York, NY 10017.

Printed in the United States of America.

Rodale Inc. makes every effort to use acid-free ♾, recycled paper ♻.

Book design by Kara Plikaitis
Hand lettering and illustrations by Nick Hensley Wagner
Photographs by Thug Kitchen

Library of Congress Cataloging-in-Publication Data is on file with the publisher.
ISBN-13: 978-1-62336-358-1 hardcover
ISBN-13: 978-1-62336-685-8 special trade edition

Distributed to the trade by Macmillan
13 15 17 19 20 18 16 14 hardcover
2 4 6 8 10 9 7 5 3 1 special trade edition

We inspire and enable people to improve their lives and the world around them.

rodalebooks.com

"The only real stumbling block is fear of failure. In cooking you've got to have a what-the-hell attitude."

—Julia Child

TRACK LIST

eat like you

give a fuck

What the FUCK is this?

This is a fucking wake-up call. This is for that section of the grocery store that you avoid. This is for drive-thru lines so long that they block traffic. This is for ketchup and pizza qualifying as fucking vegetables. This is for everyone who wants to do better but gets lost in the bullshit.

Welcome to Thug Kitchen, bitches. We're here to help. We started our website to inspire motherfuckers to eat some goddamn vegetables and adopt a healthier lifestyle. Our motto is simple:

EAT LIKE YOU GIVE A FUCK

And why not? You eat three times a day. That seems like an adequate amount of fucks to give on a daily basis. But why does the transition from the drive-thru to homemade meals seem so fucking impossible? Maybe it's because the people who tell you how to cook healthy food come off as so fucking phony. There is an aura of elitism surrounding eating well, and so many people tend to associate health with wealth. As we learned how to cook for ourselves, we couldn't identify with these beautiful bloggers in their big-ass kitchens waxing poetic about fennel pollen as they stirred up their chanterelle-studded sauces.

FUCK. ALL. THAT. We live in the real world.

We don't need theories to explain why people choose convenience foods over home-cooked meals; we've been there. We grew up like most people: Dinners never took more than 10 minutes to heat up and everything was centered around meat and slathered in cheese. We accepted the idea of eating shit because we legitimately thought it was how food was supposed to be. With our parents busy at work and our attention focused on Ninja Turtles, we didn't fucking bother to learn how to cook for ourselves. This was a time when companies were coloring ketchup purple and teal for whatever-the-fuck marketing campaign they were running. Potato chips had a goddamn disclaimer on the bag about how the oil might cause anal leakage. What the fuck, right? Those were some dark days in food. We didn't think we had enough time or money to learn how to cook real food for ourselves, so we willingly ate that fucking nonsense. So, no, we didn't grow up in wheatgrass-covered huts on some hippie commune. We are your next-door neighbors and somewhere along the way, we learned to eat right. And you can too. Virtue

untested is no virtue at all or some shit like that, right?

You might already be down with cooking, but vegetables keep getting left out of a lot of dinners. Veggies got a bad rap they are still trying to shake. We feel you. While bougie motherfuckers were starting to discover microgreens and nettles, we were still out in the land of frozen peas and iceberg lettuce. None of us really knew how to cook a vegetable so that it didn't taste like a soggy gym sock, so we just thought all veggies were bunk. Look: Cooking vegetables takes a minute and a little finesse, but it's not fucking rocket science. It's easier to sauté kale with some garlic than it is to eat pizza bites without burning the fuck out of your tongue. We just hadn't tried.

As we learned how to do all that grown-up bullshit like drive a car, pay taxes, and own a vacuum, we got to wondering why we were avoiding the kitchen and real meals. Sure, we would have to work at it and probably burn some shit and fuck up a whole dinner, but we deserved better than a pathetic Hot Pocket. Slowly but surely we started schooling ourselves on how to shop on a budget and cook simple, healthy meals. Once we got out on our own and couldn't afford cable to distract us, we really got our shit together. Our friends were impressed by even the simplest meals we made for them and all we could think was: Why doesn't everyone know how to do this? It's not that fucking hard. After plenty of practice, we are here to show you the way and save y'all some time.

We don't understand why eating real, healthy food has to be such a BIG FUCKING DEAL.

These days, trying to do right by your body and palate comes with a fuckton of baggage, but it shouldn't have to. Nobody should apologize for trying to take care of themselves or have to struggle just to get better food for their families. You don't have to be some uptown asshole to pay attention to what you eat. We've got to start taking better care of ourselves because nobody else is going to give a damn. We decided to speak up and let people know that nobody has a monopoly on the right way to eat. Consider this book our invitation to you to elevate your nutrition and kitchen game. No matter who you are or where you are from, you are welcome at our table and to this conversation about diet. Shit is about to get real. Now pull up a fucking seat.

Nobody wants to eat grass clippings and tree roots, but everybody knows that all this fast food and processed shit hasn't been doing our wallets or our waistlines any favors. You don't get to order dinner from your car and have it ready in 3 minutes without trading off some shit along the way. We really need to renegotiate this food deal, because we're all getting fucked. We can't afford the hype. These days American households spend 42 percent of their food budget on grub prepared outside their homes. It isn't a party if you do it every fucking day, right? And let's be honest, you aren't ordering the salad. All that sodium and cholesterol ain't helping anything, and your lack of fiber is going to cause serious problems for your asshole. Yeah, wake the fuck up and take this seriously. Do it for your asshole; you two have always been close.

You already know that you need to eat more goddamn vegetables. So the fuck what? Well not only are they delicious when cooked right, but they have your back as soon as you chew their asses up. Vitamins, minerals, antioxidants, fiber, and a whole lot of other tricks are packed into these miracle foods without a bunch of empty calories clogging your shit up. There isn't a plastic-wrapped meal in any drive-thru or sitting on any shelf that can step to that. The average calorie intake in the U.S. rose almost 25 percent between 1970 and 2000 and we guarantee that wasn't all broccoli and spinach. Fruits and vegetables fill you up without packing on extra baggage that your body will have to deal with later. Studies have found that people who eat more than five servings of fruits and vegetables per day have a 20 percent lower risk of coronary heart disease compared with people who ate three servings or less. How much of your plate has veggies on it now? Drop the grease-stained bag and reflect on that shit.

OK, so plant-based meals are "good" for you, but what the fuck are you going to do about it, right? We're too practical to leave you hanging like that. This shit right here is a collection of all our best-loved meals, snacks, and sides for beginning cooks all the way to people who know their way around a farmers' market. We tagged some of our recipes with info about all the nutritious shit piled in them so you can pick up some knowledge while you grub. It will be just like how you used to read the cereal box while you ate, only without all those cartoon animals that wear shirts and no pants. We are going to arm you with all the info and techniques you need to go and kick a bunch of ass on your own. We've labored over this book to help you become the baddest motherfucker in the kitchen. These pages will be your guide to some next-level skills. No lectures and no bullshit—just

some plant-based recipes with a fuckton of swearing and a dash of health advice for good measure.

We like to have a good time in the kitchen and you should too. You are going to be one clever culinary motherfucker when we are done with you.

LET'S GET TO FUCKING WORK.

congratufuckulations

In your hands you hold the first step to becoming one bad motherfucker in the kitchen. All of the general info is here in front so you get the basics down and then ease on in to the recipes. We wish we could come over and help you with dinner but you didn't invite us, so fuck you.

The first rule of *Thug Kitchen* is: Read the recipe. Second rule of *Thug Kitchen*? READ THE GODDAMN RECIPE. Be sure that you read that shit all the way through before you start to cook. Take the time to look over any details in the bigger picture that might trip you up. You can also look up anything you might have questions about before you've overcooked the dish and start to panic. Nothing is worse than getting to a crucial point in a recipe and realizing that the next thing you need is dirty in the sink, or you don't know if you can substitute rice flour for wheat flour, meanwhile you're hustling while your food is burning up. Don't just glance at a recipe and assume you've got that shit. Save yourself the stress and read the entire fucking thing. If you're a beginner, just take a goddamn minute to learn.

Pay. Fucking. Attention.

When you are measuring ingredients, double-check that shit. There's a big difference between ½ teaspoon of salt and ½ tablespoon. One is going to complete a dope dinner and the other is going to end with a plate of regret. And yeah, sometimes your measuring cups are dirty and you're tempted to eyeball measurements out of laziness. Here is a cheat sheet of what equals what so you can just use another tool instead of fucking shit up:

3 teaspoons = 1 tablespoon
2 tablespoons = ⅛ cup
4 tablespoons = ¼ cup
5 tablespoons + 1 teaspoon = ⅓ cup
2 cups = 1 pint
4 cups = 1 quart
4 quarts = 1 gallon

And did you know that liquid measurements aren't the same as dry measurements? Fucking ridiculous, right? If you try to measure out 1 cup of water in that scoop you measure flour in, it will come up short because you can't go all the way to the top without spilling. Grab one of those glass measuring cups for liquids at the store and handle your shit right. Keep the liquid stuff in the liquid measure and the dry stuff in the dry measure and you're good to fucking go.

You Do You

Now that you've got your measurements on point, you should know that recipes are just a guide. Ha. But for real, we wrote this shit so a stranger could get down on what is being served up, but you know what the fuck you like. Taste while you're cooking, not right before you are about to serve it when it's too late to change shit. If you think it needs more spices, add more spices. If it needs more salt, add some more. Shake in some hot sauce or a little pepper. You know how you like your food. Trust yourself. Just go easy because you can't take seasoning out once you add it, but you can always add more. Make these recipes your own; write on the pages if you need to. We don't give a shit. It's your book. GET FUCKING WILD.

Recipe Remix

In a bunch of places in the book we offer ideas for substitutions in case you can't find one of the ingredients, or don't want to go all the way to the store for just one fucking item. These are the most common swaps we could think of, but the options are endless. Feel free to try and mix shit up on your own, but use some goddamn sense. Out of tomato sauce? Not a problem, just . . . PUT THE FUCKING KETCHUP BACK. NO. NOT THE SAME THING. . . . Like we were saying, just throw some diced tomatoes in a blender. Think about that shit. When you are switching things out, consider how some ingredients have different cooking times, or contain more or less liquid—which can change the whole dish's taste or consistency. Also think of what role a food you're switching out plays in the dish. Is it the main ingredient? Is it a seasoning? Is it filler?

Thinking that shit through, you'll realize you can't substitute basil for spinach in a salad because spinach is a main ingredient, but you can add spinach in place of some basil when you are making pesto because that is just one flavor component. Just slow down and use some goddamn sense.

Venturing into the Unknown Unknowns

If you don't like an ingredient, say mushrooms, then don't try a recipe where the main ingredient is a motherfucking mushroom. And don't go thinking you can just leave out some core ingredient like that and the dish will still work out. That shit is not going to fly in any recipe. EVER. Either try to live your life without making that dish (be strong), or substitute something else and accept the risks. If you're going to trailblaze, then own your mistakes as much as your triumphs. Don't fucking email us when you try switching bananas out for bell peppers and you're disappointed with how it tasted.

YOU DID THAT SHIT, NOT US. Own it.

And write it down so you never fucking repeat it.

With all that said, cooking isn't fucking rocket science. You eat food every day. You should know what the fuck is going on. Just pay attention when you're cooking, trust your taste buds, don't trying adding weird shit without thinking, and you'll be fine. After you have been doing this a bit, you won't have to work so hard and dinner will take no time at all. Future you will crush it in the kitchen.

So you're ready to cook, but when you open your cupboard there's nothing but an assortment of small condiment packets collected from nearly every fast-food restaurant within a delivery radius of your place. We're going to fix that shit. Let the ketchup and soy sauce packets go now. You won't be needing them.

What the FUCK is in a THUG KITCHEN?

Basic Tools for Kitchen Domination

You need some simple tools to get the job done at dinner, but it doesn't have to be a bunch of expensive bullshit. *Oh, I need to spend 80 dollars on this Japanese ice mold because drinks taste better with round ice?* Fuck off, unnamed pricey kitchen shop. We're not buying your fuckery. Hell, you could even get a lot of the stuff on this list at a yard sale or at a dollar store. Who the fuck needs an avocado slicer? A person without any goddamn sense, that's who. Stick to this basic list and you will be set for almost anything.

Weapons of Choice

- can opener
- vegetable peeler
- measuring spoons
- measuring cups, liquid and dry
- colander
- mesh strainer (for washing/draining finer shit like rice)
- 2 cutting boards, one for vegetables and one for fruit (cutting an apple where you just cut an onion will fuck up your pie something awful. Trust.)
- large chef's knife (like 6 to 8 inches is cool. Keep this fucker sharp, too.)
- 3 bowls—large, medium, and small
- box grater
- big skillet or wok
- large soup pot
- wooden spoon
- 2 spatulas (an angled one for flipping shit like pancakes and a rubber one for batters and wet stuff)
- blender or immersion blender
- parchment paper (do not confuse this with wax paper. That will straight fuck up your meal.)
- rimmed baking sheet
- baking dish (like something you could put lasagna in)

Optional but Awesome and Helpful

- food processor (get a tiny one for $30 and chop your shit in shifts like we do.)
- small paring knife
- rolling pin
- grill pan or grill

Staples

Pantry Shit

- **olive oil:** We use extra virgin olive oil because we buy this shit by the barrel, but pure olive oil is cool, too, and cheaper.
- **neutral-tasting oil:** peanut, sesame, grapeseed, or refined coconut oil
- soy sauce or tamari
- **a couple styles of hot sauce you like:** A vinegary Southern style, an Asian style, and a taqueria-style hot sauce are a good mix to keep stocked.
- **a nut butter you like:** peanut, almond, tahini, whatever
- rice vinegar
- **one other vinegar you like:** apple cider, red wine, balsamic, white wine, whateverthefuck you find
- **your favorite grains:** We never run out of short-grain brown rice.
- **your favorite pasta noodles:** One kind of Italian-style pasta like rotini or spaghetti and some Japanese-style pastas like soba or udon are good to have on hand.
- canned diced tomatoes, no salt added
- **your favorite dried and canned beans:** We are all about cooking beans ourselves, but sometimes you get out of work late and need some help. No judgment. Stock both.
- canned/boxed veggie broth

Basic Dried Herbs and Spices

- good all-purpose, no-salt seasoning blend
- basil
- black pepper
- cayenne pepper
- chili powder
- Chinese 5-spice powder
- cinnamon
- cumin
- garlic powder (granulated garlic is cool too)
- oregano
- salt
- smoked paprika
- thyme

Vegetable Basics

- yellow onions
- bulbs of garlic
- lemons and limes
- carrots
- some kind of leafy green like spinach, kale, or lettuce

Give yourself some time and eventually you'll get all this shit. Don't stress if your kitchen doesn't look right after a month. It took us a couple years to get our kitchen cabinets on point. You will be turning out dope food in no time, even if you just have a knife, a spoon, and a bowl. We know you; you're scrappy as fuck.

<<< Staple Ingredients on Lock

You don't need to run out and blow a whole paycheck on this shit right now. Yeah it looks like a lot, but you will build up your pantry as you cook new recipes and buy a bunch of staple ingredients. The more you cook using these items, the cheaper your meals will get. Sure, you have to drop 3 dollars on a jar of ground cumin now, but you will use that shit for months and months before you have to buy it again. Look over the list at left and keep it in the back of your mind for when these fuckers go on sale.

If you're able to keep most of this shit at your place, you'll always be able to make yourself something to eat even if your fridge is looking bare.

SO HOW THE FUCK DO YOU DO THAT?

Every now and then you might want to know how to cook some basic shit without a long-ass recipe. We got you. Below we compiled all the info you need to whip up a basic batch of beans or grains without a ton of work. Flip back to this section any time you find a recipe that calls for cooked beans or suggests a side of grains. It's good to cook big batches of this shit and store them in the fridge or freezer so that dinner comes together fast when you drag your ass home from work.

Basic Pot of Beans

Throwing together a pot of beans is some of the easiest shit you can do in the kitchen. You just need some patience. The steps are the same regardless of what bean you're making, only the cooking time changes. Here are some guidelines, but trust your taste. The beans are done when at least five of them taste tender and are cooked through. One bean can be a fucking liar so taste a few. Keep simmering until you get there. Simple shit.

First, pick through the dried beans and throw out any that look fucked up, then rinse the winners. Put them in a big container and cover with a couple inches of water. They're

PASTEURIZED FOR YOUR

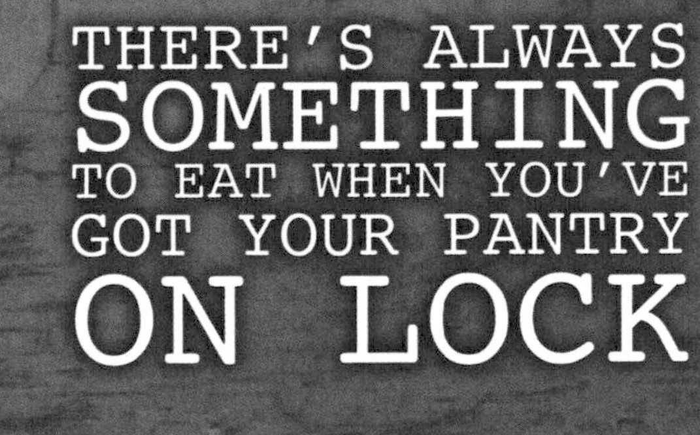
THERE'S ALWAYS
SOMETHING
TO EAT WHEN YOU'VE
GOT YOUR PANTRY
ON LOCK

going to swell up as they soak and you don't want those bastards sticking up out the water. Soak them overnight or for at least 4 hours. This will help cut down on your cook time. Throw them in the water before you go to work and then they're ready to cook when you get home.

When you're ready to cook the beans, drain the soaking water and throw the beans in a pot. You can add some carrots, onions, celery, or bay leaves for flavor, but that shit is not required. Add a bunch of fresh water, about 3 times the height of the beans in the pot. Simmer this, uncovered, until the beans are tender. Add a couple pinches of salt in the last 10 minutes of cooking for flavor. Drain any extra liquid and toss out any sad-looking veggies in the pot and store the cooked beans in the fridge or freezer until you're ready for them. No can opener required.

Here are some bean basics, but remember that shit really does change depending on how long you soaked your beans and how old they are. Math tip: Beans tend to triple in size when you cook them, so if you want to end up with 1½ cups of cooked beans (the standard can measurement), you want to start with ½ cup dried beans.

Standard cooking times for different beans

Black beans—1 to 1½ hours
Black-eyed peas—1 hour
Garbanzo beans/chickpeas (same shit) —1½ hours
Kidney and cannellini beans—1½ hours
White, great Northern, and navy beans —1 to 1½ hours
Pinto beans—1½ to 2 hours

Cooking Basic Grains

Cooking grains tends to be a lot quicker than cooking beans, but these fuckers are a little more high maintenance. Just follow these grain guides for 2 to 4 servings and you should be set up. If you ever end up with extra water in the pot when your grains are done, just drain that shit off—don't keep cooking until your grains are all mushy. Also, if you run out of water before your grains are done, just pour more in. You're not going to fuck anything up. You got this.

Barley

This grain is nutty, chewy, and fucking delicious. Not only is it full fiber, but it's packed tight with selenium, copper, and manganese so you know you are getting tons of nutritional bang for your buck.

There are 2 kinds of barley sold at most stores, hulled and pearled. Hulled takes longer to cook but has more good stuff than the pearled variety, which has had that shit polished off. Pearled barley is super creamy and easier to find in most places, so use whatever you got. For hulled barley, you want to add 1 cup of it to 3 cups of water on the stove with a pinch of salt. Bring it to a boil, cover, then simmer until that shit is tender, 40 to 50 minutes. For pearled barley, you keep the grain-to-water ratio the same but simmer it uncovered and start checking to see if it's tender after 20 to 25 minutes.

Couscous

This cooks quick since technically it's a pasta, not a grain. Look that shit up. Anyway, these tiny bastards will be ready in 10 minutes flat. Throw a cup of couscous in a pot with a lid and a pinch of salt. Add 1¼ cups boiling water, stir, and throw the lid on. No heat under the pot or anything. Let that sit for 8 minutes, then fluff the couscous with a fork and serve. Fucking done.

Millet

Millet might look like birdseed, but it deserves more love in the kitchen and is cheap as hell. It's kinda like a mix between quinoa and brown rice and worthy of a test run on your plate. Throw 1 cup of millet in a medium pot over medium heat and sauté it around until it smells toasty, about 2 minutes. Add 2 cups of water and a pinch of salt and simmer that shit, covered, until the millet is tender, 25 to 35 minutes.

Quinoa

Some people cook this protein-packed seed like rice, but others treat it like pasta. Whatthefuckever you prefer, make sure to rinse these little fuckers before you throw them in to cook, otherwise they can taste bitter. To cook, bring 2 cups water to boil in a medium stock pot with a pinch of salt, drop in the quinoa and simmer, uncovered, for 15 to 20 minutes or until the quinoa is tender. Drain away any water that's left.

Brown Rice

You might think this is some hippie health food, but it brings way more nutrition and flavor to the table than white rice. We always have some in the fridge, and your ass should, too. If you're still giving this motherfucker the side eye, try out the short grain variety (below). That nutty, delicious motherfucker will make you forget white rice altogether. You can cook the long grain variety in the same way, but know that shit will take about 15 minutes longer and an extra ½ cup of water.

BASIC BIG POT OF BROWN RICE

Serve alongside all kinds of good shit like the Mango Curry (page 158), or as a base in a bowl (see How to Build a Bowl, page 174).

MAKES 4 CUPS

1 teaspoon olive or coconut oil*
2 cups short-grain brown rice
Pinch of salt
3½ cups water

1 In a medium saucepan, heat the oil over medium heat. Add the rice and sauté that shit until it smells a little nutty, about 2 minutes. Add the salt and water and stir. Bring to a simmer, then reduce the heat, cover, and let this very softly simmer until all the water is absorbed and the rice is tender, about 35 minutes.

2 Did you fuck up the heat and the rice is tender but there's still water? Just fucking drain it. Or is the rice not done but all the water is gone? Just stir in a little more water, turn the heat down, and keep going. Don't let some rice shake your game.

* *This step with the oil is optional, but it gives the rice a nuttier taste so it's fucking delicious. Your call.*

FOOD

HOLD THE FUCK UP, WHERE'S THE MEAT?

If you've flipped through these pages or been on our site, you might have noticed that our recipes don't use meat. Actually, our recipes don't call for any animal products at all. We know this might be weird at first, but just fucking hear us out. According to the Food and Agriculture Organization of the United Nations, Americans on average eat 270 pounds of meat a year. That is more than double the USDA recommended maximum protein consumption of 125 pounds per year. Basically, most of us are eating entirely too much meat and not mixing up our protein sources at all. So come the fuck on, the last thing anybody needs is another book coming out telling you how to cook meat. Clearly you got that shit on lock.

Eating all that meat and other animal products like cheese and eggs—while neglecting the fuck out of fruit, vegetables, and whole grains—does come with consequences. You saw that shit coming. You know about your cholesterol levels and all that, but you have a lot more to look out for. Researchers at the University of Southern California found that people with diets rich in animal proteins were four times more likely than those who ate less of it to die of cancer. They followed thousands of people for 20 years and also found that those same animal protein-loving motherfuckers were 74 percent more likely to die OF ANY CAUSE, not just cancer, during the course of the study than people with a diet low in shit like meat, cheese, and eggs. Yeah, for real. Maybe it is time to rethink what kinds of foods we eat on the regular.

You think you can't live without meat every fucking day? Well guess what? You can't live *with* that shit either, at least not for as long as you should. Eating more plant-based meals will not only safeguard your health, but it is a great way to get out of your dinner rut. We know you have been making the same five things for dinner for years. Time to drop some of that meat, cheese, and eggs and mix shit up. Eat like you give a fuck and your whole body will thank you. Now let's get to it.

COFFEE

carpe
fucking
diem

BREAKFAST

IT'S TOO EARLY TO BE AN ASSHOLE

SERIOUSLY, YOU NEED TO EAT BREAKFAST

You've heard the same shit a million times, but it's true: Breakfast is the most important meal of the day. Consider the fact that when you wake up, you haven't eaten anything for 6 to 8 hours—sometimes longer, depending on whatever the fuck you justified as last night's dinner. So you really think it's OK to coast on fumes until lunch? Skipping breakfast is not only lazy but that shit is detrimental to your health. The Harvard School of Public Health found that regularly skipping breakfast increases the risk of a heart attack and heart disease by over 25 percent. Yeah, "oh fuck" would be an accurate reaction.

When lunchtime comes around, if you've eaten breakfast, you'll make smarter decisions instead of desperately inhaling the first edible thing you can wrap your hungry hands on, causing your blood sugar to spike. It's dumb shit like that that leads to diabetes, high blood pressure, and high cholesterol, so keep that blood sugar in check with your morning meals. Breakfast is also a way to get your daily dose of fiber to keep you feeling full. Eat well, eat small meals, and eat often and you won't have to apologize for your shitty attitude or for eating a whole large pizza by yourself.

Oh, you don't have time, or you're not hungry when you wake up? What a unique fucking excuse. Breakfast doesn't take a shitload of time. Sure, there is a whole chapter here with some badass breakfast foods, but do you know what else makes a respectable breakfast? Cold leftovers, which take seconds to eat. Anyone who says you can't have spaghetti for breakfast is a hater. And since when did not being hungry stop you from eating? Ever eat chips by the handful because you're just fucking bored? Yet some toast with peanut butter on it at 7:30 a.m. is just too much to deal with? Don't fucking give us that.

QUINOA OATMEAL

The fiber in the oatmeal helps control your blood sugar and keeps you feeling full until lunch. The quinoa gives your morning a little extra protein because why the fuck not? Start your day right by owning the shit out of it. Serve the oatmeal with fresh fruit, nuts, maple syrup, brown sugar, whateverthefuck will get you through your day.

MAKES ENOUGH FOR 4

4 cups water
½ cup quinoa
1 teaspoon olive or coconut oil
1 cup steel-cut oats
Pinch of salt
½ cup almond milk

1 Heat up the water in a kettle on the stovetop or in the microwave until it is near boiling. Put the quinoa in a strainer and rinse that shit so it isn't bitter after you cook it.

2 In a saucepan, heat the oil over medium heat. Add the oats and stir them around until they smell kinda toasty, about 2 minutes. Add the quinoa and the hot water and bring it all to a boil. This won't take long because the water should already be hot as fuck.

3 Once it is boiling, turn down the heat on the pot and let it simmer uncovered. Go check your tumblr or Facebook shit while it cooks for 25 to 30 minutes. It should taste done now, not hard but still a little chewy. Add the almond milk and turn off the heat.

4 Love to hit snooze? Double the recipe and heat up the leftovers all week.

MIXED VEGGIE AND TOFU CHILAQUILES

This dish makes for a hearty breakfast the morning after a big party. If your head is still pounding and your stomach is grumbling, chilaquiles will set your ass straight.

MAKES ENOUGH FOR 4 TO 6

12 corn tortillas
2 teaspoons olive oil
1 block medium-firm tofu*
2 teaspoons soy sauce or tamari
1 teaspoon garlic powder
¼ cup nutritional yeast ("nooch")**
½ medium onion, chopped
1 red, orange, or green bell pepper, chopped
1 to 2 jalapeños, chopped
2 cloves garlic, minced
2 to 3 cups fresh spinach
2½ cups salsa verde***
¼ cup vegetable broth or water
Toppings: avocado, cilantro, jalapeños, pico de gallo

* *You want the kind packed in water that is sold in the fridge at the store, so make sure to drain that shit before you start cooking.*

** *WTF? See page 10.*

*** *See page 126 for a recipe, or you could buy that shit if you are feeling super lazy.*

1 Crank your oven to 400°F. Cut your tortillas up into 8 wedges, like a motherfucking pizza. Spread the wedges out on a baking sheet and throw them in the oven for 15 to 20 minutes to dry out. Stir them around halfway through. It's fine if they start to get hard in some spots but don't let them fucking burn.

2 While the tortillas get crispy, grab a big skillet and do the damn thing. Heat up 1 teaspoon of the oil over a medium heat and crumble in the tofu. It might be a little watery, but don't worry about that shit. Think runny scrambled eggs. Stir in the soy sauce and garlic powder and let it all cook together until some of that water cooks off, about 2 minutes. Stir in the nooch, turn off the heat, and pour the tofu into a bowl. Wipe the skillet down and throw that motherfucker right back on the stove cause we ain't done yet.

3 Heat up that second teaspoon of oil over medium heat. Throw in the onion, bell pepper, and jalapeños and sauté until the onion starts to look a little brown, 3 to 5 minutes. Add the garlic and spinach and cook for 30 seconds more.

4 The baked tortillas should be done now, so throw about half of them in with the veggies in the skillet. Add 1 cup of the salsa and 2 tablespoons of the broth and mix all of that together. Add half of the tofu over the whole skillet and then layer on the rest of the tortillas. Top with the rest of the tofu, salsa, and broth and gently stir it around to make sure the layers are coated. A dry bite of chilaquiles can be a fucking bummer, so pay attention. Let this all simmer together for about 5 minutes so that the tortillas soften up and the liquid evaporates. The dope smell of cooking this will drag even the laziest motherfucker out of bed. Believe that shit.

5 Serve right away topped with sliced avocado, a sprinkle of cilantro, more jalapeños, and pico de gallo. Don't share until someone else promises to wash the goddamn dishes.

BASIC MAPLE GRANOLA
WITH ADD-IN IDEAS

Most store-bought granola is more sugar than oats. Why not just buy a jar of sprinkles for your breakfast and save yourself the trouble? If you want sweetness with some bulk behind it, make this granola and see what the fuck you've been missing.

MAKES A LITTLE MORE THAN 5 CUPS

3 cups rolled oats
½ cup sunflower seeds*
½ cup chopped almonds*
¼ cup uncooked millet**
½ cup maple syrup***
⅓ cup olive oil
½ teaspoon vanilla extract
½ teaspoon ground cinnamon
½ teaspoon salt
½ cup dried cranberries ** (optional)**

1 Heat your oven to 300°F. Line a rimmed baking sheet with some parchment paper.

2 Mix together the oats, seeds, nuts, and millet in a large bowl.

3 In a medium glass, stir together the maple syrup, oil, and vanilla. Pour this all over the oat mixture and stir that shit around until everything looks coated. Add the cinnamon and the salt and stir.

4 Pour all of this evenly over that baking sheet and stick it in the oven for 40 minutes. Stir it every 10 minutes so that it cooks evenly. You'll know this shit is done when everything looks kinda toasted and the oats feel crispy instead of damp. Stir in the dried fruit now if you're using any. Let that all cool on the baking sheet and then store it in an airtight container for up to 2 weeks.

5 Want to mix it up? Try these nut and fruit combos: almonds and chopped, dried apricots or strawberries; walnuts and dried pears or figs; pecans and dried cherries; peanuts and dried apples or bananas. Just use whateverthefuck sounds good to you.

* *Basically, 1 cup of whatever nuts you prefer.*

** *No millet? Fuck it, just add more oats.*

*** *Legit syrup can get kinda fucking expensive. But so can granola. Save up for the good shit.*

**** *Or use any dried fruit you like.*

BREAKFAST GREENS

This single-pan side has everything your sleepy ass needs in the morning. This goes great with Biscuits and Gravy (page 18) if you've got some fucking time.

MAKES ENOUGH FOR 2 TO 4 AS A SIDE

- **¼ cup vegetable broth**
- **1½ teaspoons maple syrup or agave syrup**
- **1 teaspoon tomato paste**
- **1 teaspoon liquid smoke***
- **2 teaspoons soy sauce, tamari, or Bragg's Liquid Aminos***
- **2 teaspoons olive or grapeseed oil**
- **8 ounces tempeh**
- **2 cloves garlic, minced**
- **1½ teaspoons of your favorite no-salt, all-purpose seasoning blend**
- **1 bunch kale, cut into 2-inch strips (about 7 cups)**
- **2 tablespoons lemon juice**

1 In a small glass, mix together the broth, maple syrup, tomato paste, liquid smoke, and 1 teaspoon of the soy sauce and set that shit aside.

2 Heat the oil in a big wok or skillet over medium heat. Crumble in the tempeh in bite-size pieces and sauté it around until it starts to brown in some places, 2 to 3 minutes. Now pour that broth mixture all over and let it cook for about 15 seconds. Add the garlic and seasoning blend and cook for another 30 seconds. Almost done.

3 Now we get to the greens. Pile those motherfuckers on top of the tempeh, pour in the lemon juice and remaining 1 teaspoon soy sauce, and stir everything around with the tempeh. It will look like too much kale but respect the process, damn. Let the kale cook down for about a minute or two—you want it nice and wilted, not cooked to death. Serve right away.

***** *WTF? See page 10.*

TOFU SCRAMBLE TACOS

Serve with avocados, fresh cilantro, and your favorite salsa. Fuck yeah.

MAKES ABOUT 8 TACOS

- 1 small crown broccoli
- 1 red bell pepper
- 1 yellow onion
- 1 carrot
- 4 cloves garlic
- 1 to 2 jalapeños*
- 1 tablespoon ground cumin
- 1 tablespoon chili powder
- 2 teaspoons dried oregano
- 2 teaspoons olive oil
- 1 block extra-firm tofu
- 2 to 3 teaspoons soy sauce, tamari, or Bragg's**
- 2 tablespoons lemon or lime juice
- ⅓ cup nutritional yeast**
- 2 teaspoons of your favorite hot sauce
- 8 corn or flour tortillas, warmed

1 Chop up the broccoli into pieces no larger than a nickel, aiming for about 2 cups. Dice the bell pepper and onion into pea-size pieces. Shred the carrot on that box grater you think you bought a while back. Mince the garlic and jalapeño. In a small bowl, mix together the cumin, chili powder, and oregano and set that shit aside. PREP WORK, MOTHERFUCKER.

2 Now it's time to cook. In a large skillet, heat the oil over medium heat. Add the onion and cook until it starts to look golden around the edges, 3 to 5 minutes. Now add the chopped broccoli and bell pepper and cook until the broccoli starts to get tender but isn't all fucking limp, another 3 to 4 minutes. Don't overcook this shit or your broccoli will taste like little soggy trees. Now add the garlic and jalapeño and sauté for about 30 seconds.

3 While that shit is going on, drain the tofu and squeeze out as much water as possible. (You can just use your hands; no need to press this bastard.) Now crumble that tofu into the pan in quarter-size chunks. Some small bits are cool but the more you stir it, the more shit is going to break down, so its better to start bigger and work to smaller, you know? Sauté that tofu around with the veggies for 2 to 3 minutes and try to get it all mixed in. If the pan starts looking dry, add a splash of water and move the fuck on. Add the soy sauce and lemon/lime juice all over the pan. Add the spice blend, shredded carrot, and nutritional yeast right after and stir those fuckers in. Let this all cook together for about 2 minutes so that the flavors blend. Top with the hot sauce, stir, and then pile the filling into your waiting tortillas. Breakfast is served, bitches.

* *Whatever heat you can handle. Remove the seeds for less heat.*

** *WTF? See page 10.*

START EVERY DAMN DAY LIKE IT'S
TACO TUESDAY

DROPPING KNOWLEDGE

WEIRD FUCKING INGREDIENTS

<<< NOOCH

Nutritional yeast, or *nooch* if you are in the know, is some level 7 hippie shit. It's deactivated yeast sold in flakes that makes everything taste kinda cheesy. It's like healthy Cheeto dust. The future is now, people. It's packed with B_{12}, folic acid, selenium, zinc, and some protein. You can find it in bulk bins at some grocery stores and on the fucking Internet. It is not the same thing as brewer's yeast, and anybody who tells you otherwise is a goddamn liar.

BRAGG'S LIQUID AMINOS

You can usually find this old-school sauce near the vinegars or soy sauces in the healthy eating section of most big grocery stores and on the Internet. Obvs. It tastes a lot like soy sauce but with a little something extra. If you can't find it, just sub with soy sauce or tamari.

LIQUID SMOKE

This flavor enhancer is made by collecting the smoke from wood chips, letting it cool, and adding some water. It adds a fuckton of flavor, but a little goes a long way. Don't overdo it. It is near the BBQ sauce at the store, we swear. You haven't even looked yet so stop fucking complaining.

BROWN RICE BOWL WITH EDAMAME AND TAMARI SCALLION SAUCE

Savory food for breakfast is the shit and more people need to hop on board. This basic breakfast bowl is habit-forming, so watch the fuck out. The brown rice is super filling and the edamame brings plenty of protein to the table, so you'll feel like a fucking champ.

MAKES ENOUGH FOR 4 TO 6

TAMARI SCALLION SAUCE

- 1 cup sliced green onions*
- ¼ cup rice vinegar
- 2 tablespoons orange juice
- 4 teaspoons toasted sesame oil
- 1 teaspoon tamari or soy sauce

- Basic Big Pot of Brown Rice (page xxiv)
- 4 cups shelled edamame**
- ⅓ cup sliced almonds, toasted (optional)

1 Make the sauce: Throw everything into a food processor or blender and let it run until the sauce looks sorta smooth. You should get about ⅔ cup of sauce.

2 To assemble the bowl, spoon equal parts brown rice and edamame into a bowl and drizzle a tablespoon or two of sauce all over it. If you aren't super hungry in the mornings, ½ cup of each should do you. If you want some added crunch, sprinkle some sliced almonds over the top. You can make this shit all on Sunday night and then just heat it up all week for breakfast.

* *Green onions, scallions . . . they're the same damn thing. "Scallion" just sounds more legit next to the word "sauce."*

** *Edamame are immature soybeans and are tasty as fuck. They have a great texture and are full of good shit like protein, fatty acids, and tons of fiber. Find them in the frozen veggie section at the store and keep your freezer full.*

MAKE YOUR OWN PANCAKE MIX

Don't want to measure out a bunch of shit every time you make pancakes? We get that. But don't go out buying that overpriced, sugar-filled boxed bullshit. Just take a couple minutes and make a big batch for yourself and keep it in your pantry for the next time you're jonesing for flapjacks.

This is going to require some basic math, so hold tight. From the Whole Wheat Banana Pancake recipe (opposite), we know that 1 batch of 12 pancakes takes approximately $2\frac{2}{3}$ cups dry ingredients. Cool. Now decide how many batches of pancake mix you want to store away for later. Five? Ten? It doesn't really fucking matter, just multiply all the dry ingredient amounts in the recipe by that number and measure them out into a large bowl. Whisk them all together, making sure everything is well distributed, then pour this mix into a large airtight container. Mix made, motherfucker.

Next time you want pancakes, reach into that container and measure out $2\frac{2}{3}$ cups of the dry mix, then add the 2 cups of milk and 1 mashed banana and follow the rest of recipe. Simple shit. Only want 6 pancakes? Measure out $1\frac{1}{3}$ cups of dry mix and add 1 cup of milk and half a banana. You can do this ALL. FUCKING. DAY. Just keep the ratio of dry ingredients to wet the same and you'll have pancakes in no time. (If you hate bananas, you could sub in $\frac{1}{4}$ cup more liquid, but it won't taste as dope.)

WHOLE WHEAT BANANA PANCAKES

Serve these warm with legit maple syrup (none of that fake-ass corn syrup) and some fresh fruit on the side. You know how to eat a fucking pancake.

MAKES ABOUT 12 PANCAKES, WHICH YOU CAN FREEZE AND EAT WHENEVERTHEFUCK YOU WANT

2½ cups whole wheat pastry flour or all-purpose flour

2 tablespoons brown or white sugar

2 teaspoons baking soda

½ teaspoon salt

2 cups nondairy milk (like almond)

1 small banana, mashed *

Grapeseed oil or coconut oil for cooking the pancakes

1 In a big bowl, whisk together the flour, sugar, baking soda, and salt. Make a crater in the middle and add the milk and mashed up banana. Mix that all together until there are no more dry spots, but don't go crazy. Mixing it too much will make your pancakes tough, so just chill the fuck out sir mix-a-lot.

2 Now, you probably know what to do once the batter is done, but in case this is your first time at the griddle, keep reading. Grab a skillet or griddle and heat it over medium heat. Lightly grease the pan with some oil and pour some pancake batter onto the griddle for each pancake you want. Cook the first side for about 2 minutes or until bubbles appear on top. The bubbles mean your pancake has cooked through. Flip and continue cooking the other side for 1 to 2 minutes or until the pancake looks golden brown.

* *This should be around ⅓ cup.*

STOP FUCKING WITH THAT FROZEN AISLE SHIT

FRESH WAFFLES OR NO WAFFLES

CORNMEAL WAFFLES WITH STRAWBERRY SYRUP

The cornmeal in these motherfuckers gives a little something extra that sets the gold standard in the waffle game.

MAKES ABOUT 4 BIG-ASS WAFFLES, BUT THIS VARIES DEPENDING ON YOUR WAFFLE MAKER

STRAWBERRY SYRUP

- 1 pound strawberries*
- 2 to 4 tablespoons sugar**
- 1/4 cup orange juice
- 1/2 teaspoon vanilla extract

WAFFLES

- 2 cups almond or your favorite nondairy milk
- 1 teaspoon apple cider vinegar or lemon juice
- 1 1/2 cups cornmeal***
- 1 cup all-purpose or whole wheat flour
- 2 tablespoons brown sugar
- 1 1/2 tablespoons baking powder
- 1/2 teaspoon salt
- 1/8 teaspoon ground cinnamon
- 2 tablespoons oil (grapeseed, olive, or safflower would work)
- Cooking spray

1 First, make that sweet syrup: Cut the stems off the strawberries and chop the berries into bean-size pieces. Throw them in a small saucepan with the rest of the syrup ingredients and warm it all over a medium-low heat. At first it might not look like there's enough liquid in this bitch to make syrup, but once everything gets going the strawberries will fix that shit. Trust. Stir it around and bring it to a gentle simmer. Let it go for 15 to 20 minutes, stirring every minute or so, until the syrup thickens up and the liquids begin to evaporate. Turn off the heat.

2 While your syrup is cooling, make your waffles: Heat up the waffle iron. Mix together the milk and vinegar in a small glass and set it aside. In a large bowl, whisk together the cornmeal, flour, brown sugar, baking powder, salt, and cinnamon so that they are all combined. Make a crater in the center and add the milk mixture and the oil. Whisk everything together until there aren't any more dry spots and only a few lumps. Coat the plates of the preheated waffle iron with some cooking spray so those bitches won't stick, then pour in some batter. Cook until golden brown according to your waffle maker's directions. Cover with strawberry syrup and serve hot.

* *Fresh strawberries are best but frozen will do as long as you thaw that shit out.*

** *Add the 4 tablespoons if your strawberries aren't that sweet or if you like a sweet-ass syrup.*

*** *Same shit that you would use to make cornbread. Sometimes it's called corn flour in the store. Just don't buy polenta and you'll be cool.*

TO-GO BREAKFAST BARS

Some mornings you've just got to get the fuck out the door. We know that I'm-running-so-goddamn-late hustle. Be proactive and make this shit on the weekend so your slacking ass can grab one on your way out.

MAKES ABOUT 10 BARS

- **2 cups rolled oats**
- **¾ cup uncooked quinoa**
- **¼ cup uncooked millet**
- **1¼ cups chopped mixed nuts or seeds***
- **½ cup dried cranberries or similar dried fruit**
- **¼ teaspoon salt**
- **½ cup maple syrup**
- **½ cup peanut or almond butter**
- **¼ cup refined coconut oil or olive oil**
- **2 tablespoons white or brown sugar**
- **1 teaspoon vanilla extract**

1 Heat your oven to 350°F. Grab a 9 x 13-inch baking dish and line it with parchment so some of the paper goes over the edge of the pan. This makes it way fucking easier to just lift the bars out of the pan after they cool. Planning ahead like a fucking grownup.

2 Heat a large skillet or wok over a medium-low heat and add the oats, quinoa, and millet. Stir them all around until they start to smell toasted, about 3 minutes. While that shit is happening, combine the nuts and cranberries in a large bowl. Pour in the toasted oat mix and the salt and mix that shit together.

3 In a small saucepan, combine the maple syrup, peanut butter, oil, sugar, and vanilla and warm until everything is melted. Make sure that the peanut butter is all mixed and then remove from the heat. Pour this all over the dry mix and stir until everything is fucking coated.

4 Pour the mixture into the baking dish and press it down with a spoon to even it out and make sure it is really fucking in there. Throw it in the oven until it all looks toasted, 25 to 30 minutes. Let it cool to room temperature in the pan then throw it into the fridge. When it's all nice and cold, cut into bars. They keep best in the fridge.

***** *We like ½ cup pumpkin seeds, ½ cup sunflower seeds, and ½ cup sliced almonds but mix it up how you like.*

WHOLE WHEAT BISCUITS

Make your own biscuits because that store-bought shit is shady as hell. Food shouldn't be packaged like a stick of explosives. That shit is unnatural.

MAKES ABOUT 8 BISCUITS

1 cup almond or other nondairy milk
½ teaspoon apple cider vinegar
1½ cups whole wheat pastry flour*
1 cup all-purpose flour**
1 tablespoon baking powder
2 teaspoons sugar
½ teaspoon salt
¼ cup solid refined coconut oil***

1 Crank your oven to 425°F. Line a baking sheet with some parchment paper.

2 Mix together the milk and vinegar in a small glass and set it out of the way for a minute.

3 Sift the flours, baking powder, sugar, and salt together in a medium bowl. Crumble the oil into the flour a tablespoon at a time using your fingers and break up into pieces a little bigger than a pea. It should look kinda like coarse sand from a shitty playground, minus the broken glass. Make a well in the center and pour in the milk mixture. Stir until a shaggy dough is formed, but be careful not to overmix because then you will have some tough biscuits. If it is too dry to stick together, add a tablespoon or two of milk.

4 Turn the dough out on a floured surface and pat it into a roughly 8 x 5-inch rectangle about 1½ inches thick. Using the open end of a glass or biscuit cutter, cut out all the motherfucking biscuits you can and put them on the baking sheet. You should end up with about 8.

5 Bake the biscuits until the bottoms are golden, 15 to 18 minutes. Let them cool for a minute before digging in or go ahead and start the day by burning the fuck out of your taste buds, you dumbass.

* *Whole wheat pastry flour is really similar to all-purpose flour in texture and taste but contains all the good bran and germ stuff like you find in whole wheat flour. Basically, it is the shit. If you can't find it, use whole wheat or all-purpose instead.*

** *Yeah, don't bitch. In the quest for a fluffy biscuit, it had to be done.*

*** *This needs to be all opaque and solid like butter. If it is clear and runny because it is hot outside, this won't fucking work. Stick it in the fridge until it gets its act together.*

BISCUITS AND GRAVY

We threw the recipe in the breakfast section, but let's get real—any time is a good time for biscuits and gravy. Serve it up with a side of Breakfast Greens (page 7) to really fill out your plate.

MAKES ENOUGH FOR 4 TO 6

LENTIL GRAVY

1½ cups green or brown lentils
5 cups water
Salt
½ small onion, diced
1 teaspoon olive oil
1 teaspoon dried thyme
2 cloves garlic, minced
⅛ teaspoon ground pepper
1 tablespoon flour
1 cup vegetable broth
1 teaspoon soy sauce or tamari
1 teaspoon paprika
½ teaspoon sherry or red wine vinegar

Whole Wheat Biscuits (page 17)

1 Make the gravy: In a pot, bring the lentils, water, and a pinch of salt to a boil. Let those bitches simmer until they are tender and kinda falling apart, about 40 minutes. Prep everything else while you wait or you can do this shit the night before and refrigerate.

2 In a small skillet, sauté the onion in the olive oil over medium heat until golden around the edges, about 3 minutes. Add the thyme, garlic, and pepper and cook for another 30 seconds. Turn off the heat.

3 When the lentils are done, drain them of whatever water is left in there and throw them back in the pot you cooked them in. In a small bowl, mix the flour into the broth. Then add the broth mixture to the lentils along with the onions, soy sauce, paprika, and vinegar. Grab an immersion blender and blend until smooth or throw it all in a regular blender and go to town. Heat it all back up on the stove in that pot again and let it simmer to thicken, 2 to 3 minutes.

4 Split the warm biscuits in half and spoon some gravy all over them. Serve right away.

THIS IS THE KIND OF
BREAKFAST
TO START A
MOTHERFUCKING
WEEKEND

OAT FLOUR GRIDDLE CAKES WITH BLUEBERRY SAUCE

Having a hard time choosing oatmeal or pancakes for breakfast? Fuck it, HAVE BOTH.

MAKES 8 TO 10 GRIDDLE CAKES

- 1½ cups rolled oats*
- 2 tablespoons ground flaxseed
- 1½ cups plain almond or other nondairy milk
- ½ cup oat flour**
- 1 tablespoon sugar
- 1½ teaspoons baking powder
- ½ teaspoon salt
- ½ teaspoon ground cinnamon
- Grapeseed or refined coconut oil, for cooking
- Blueberry Sauce (recipe opposite)

1 In a large bowl, mix together the oats, ground flaxseed, and almond milk. Stir well to make sure everything is covered and then let it sit for 10 minutes so that those oats soften up.

2 In a small bowl, mix together the flour, sugar, baking powder, salt, and cinnamon. Stir the flour mixture into the wet oats and mix until all that shit is combined.

3 Now it's time to cook these fuckers. Grab a skillet or griddle and heat it over medium heat. Lightly grease the pan with some oil and pour some of the thick batter onto the griddle for each cake. Cook the first side until the bottom looks golden brown and you can smell the toasted oats, about 2 minutes. Flip and continue cooking the other side until the cake looks golden brown all over, 1 to 2 minutes. Serve warm with some blueberry sauce for a great fucking time.

* *Not that instant bullshit. Real rolled oats.*

** *This might sound fancy, but take some rolled oats, throw them in a blender or food processor, and run until that shit looks like flour. You can use all-purpose or whole wheat flour here too if it's too early to be fucking with your blender.*

BLUEBERRY SAUCE

Serve this blueberry sauce over these griddle cakes, instead of the strawberry syrup for the Cornmeal Waffles (page 15), or swirled into your Maple Berry Grits (page 24). It's some choose-your-own-adventure-type shit.

MAKES ABOUT 1 CUP

- **½ pound fresh or frozen blueberries**
- **2 tablespoons sugar**
- **1 tablespoon lemon juice**
- **1 tablespoon water**
- **1 teaspoon vanilla extract**
- **2 large pieces lemon zest***

Throw everything together in a small saucepan over medium-low heat. It may not look like enough liquid, but once the berries start breaking down you'll see what the fuck is up. Stir it around, smashing some berries with your spoon as you go. Bring the pot to a simmer and let it go for about 10 minutes so the berries really break down and the sauce thickens a bit. Take out the lemon zest, pour the sauce into a glass or bowl, and let that shit cool for 5 to 10 minutes. It will get thicker as it cools.

* *Take your knife or sharp vegetable peeler and run it down the side of a lemon to cut off 2 pieces of the zest (the colored outer layer) about the length of a finger. Try not to get a bunch of that white shit, but don't worry too much about it.*

THERE AIN'T
NO SHAME
IN THIS
BREAKFAST
GAME

SOURDOUGH FRENCH TOAST

Who the fuck wouldn't like fried bread served with some maple syrup and fresh fruit? This shit sells itself.

MAKES 6 PIECES OF FRENCH TOAST, BUT IT'S EASY AS HELL TO DOUBLE OR TRIPLE

1 In a pie pan or similar shallow dish, mix together the ground chia seeds and flour. Slowly whisk in the milk so that shit doesn't get all lumpy. SLOWLY, MOTHERFUCKER. Now let that sit for 15 minutes. Make your sleepy ass some coffee and then cut the bread up into 1-inch-thick slices while you wait.

2 Whisk the batter after about 15 minutes and then slowly add the nutritional yeast and stir. Heat a griddle or heavy pan over a medium heat and coat with a little cooking spray so these bitches don't stick. Soak your bread slices in the batter for a couple seconds on each side and then throw them right on the griddle. Cook for 1 to 2 minutes a side, or until they look golden and tasty as fuck all over.

* *But for real, you can use whatever flour you use to bake—brown rice, all-purpose . . . it won't make a difference.*

** *Almond milk is always advised but use what you got.*

*** *WTF? See page 10.*

1½ teaspoons ground chia or flaxseeds

2 tablespoons whole wheat flour*

1 cup vanilla nondairy milk**

½ loaf day-old sourdough bread or whatever crusty bread you have lying around

1½ tablespoons nutritional yeast***

Cooking spray

MAPLE BERRY GRITS

Grits don't get enough love at breakfast. They are creamy, slightly sweet, and full of fiber. You've had enough oatmeal; it's about damn time to try something new.

MAKES ENOUGH FOR 4, OR A SOLID SOLO BREAKFAST FOR 4 DAYS

- 2 cups water
- 2 cups almond or other nondairy milk
- 1 cup stoneground grits*
- ¼ to ½ teaspoon salt
- 1 to 2 teaspoons maple syrup or your favorite liquid sweetener
- Your favorite jam
- Fresh berries

1 Grab a medium saucepan and bring the water and milk to a boil over medium heat. Gently whisk in the grits and ¼ teaspoon salt. Don't just dump it all in and spill water everywhere—show some fucking care, man. Bring it all to a boil and then reduce that heat to low. Cover the pot and then let that deliciousness simmer for 20 minutes. Stir the fucker on occasion while you sip your coffee and troll the Internet, 'cause you don't want anything sticking to the bottom.

2 When the grits have absorbed most of the liquid and are tender, turn that flame off and add 1 teaspoon of maple syrup. Taste and add the rest of the salt and syrup if you think it needs it. That's on you. Serve with a small scoop of your favorite jam on top and some fresh berries so it looks all classy as fuck.

* *Not that instant bullshit.*

GRAB TODAY BY THE GRITS

BAKED OKRA AND POTATO HASH

It's a damn shame if you haven't tried okra and potatoes together for breakfast. Hurry the fuck up and right this wrong.

MAKES ENOUGH FOR 2 TO 3 AS A SIDE

- Cooking spray
- 1 pound yellow or red potatoes
- ½ yellow onion
- 1 pound okra
- 2 teaspoons olive oil
- 2 tablespoons cornmeal
- Dash of ground pepper
- ¼ teaspoon salt
- ½ teaspoon paprika
- 2 cloves garlic, minced
- 1½ teaspoons minced fresh rosemary
- 1 tablespoon lemon juice
- Hot sauce, for serving

1 Crank your oven to 425°F. Lightly coat a large rimmed baking sheet with cooking spray.

2 Chop the potatoes into pieces about the size of a nickel (skins and all if you can hang), chop up the onion, and slice the okra into ¼-inch pieces. Okra can be kinda slimy when you cut it up. Just deal with it and fucking move on. In a medium bowl, toss together 1 teaspoon of the olive oil and the sliced okra. Mix well. Add the cornmeal, pepper, and ⅛ teaspoon of the salt and mix again. The cornmeal will make the okra less slimy; trust. Pour all that onto half of the baking sheet.

3 Throw the potato and onion into the bowl that just held the okra. Add the last 1 teaspoon oil, the paprika, and last ⅛ teaspoon salt and mix it up. Pour this onto the other half of the baking sheet and put that motherfucker in the oven. After about 20 minutes, add the garlic and rosemary to the potato side of the sheet and stir that up. Stir the okra around too and put that fucker right back in the oven to finish cooking. Bake until the okra starts to brown and crisp up, another 20 to 25 minutes.

4 When the okra is crispy and the potatoes are browned and tender, take it out of the oven and sprinkle the lemon juice over the entire dish. Mix the potatoes and okra together and serve immediately with your favorite hot sauce.

GREEN SMOOTHIES SHOULDN'T TASTE LIKE GRASS

Green smoothies are an easy way to get more fruits and veggies into your diet. You can get a dose of fiber, chlorophyll, essential vitamins, and all kinds of other good stuff your body needs in one glass. That is some simple shit. Don't overthink it.

The greens lay the nutritional groundwork while the sweetness from the fruit handles the flavor labor. But don't go to some buttoned-up juice bar across town for an expensive-ass neon green smoothie that tastes like grass clippings. FUCK. THAT. Toss some fruits and veggies in a blender and press a fucking button. You know what you like, so be your own green smoothie guru at home. It's faster, cheaper, and no long-ass line. Here's a guide to how you want to structure your smoothie experiments:

2 cups of greens like spinach or kale, whatever you got. (If you have a shitty blender, stick to something easier to blend, like spinach.)

1 cup chunks of creamy fruit (like frozen bananas or mangoes or an avocado)

$\frac{3}{4}$ cup of your favorite sweet frozen fruits (like cherries, berries, apples, pears—use your fucking imagination)

$1\frac{1}{2}$ cups liquid. This can be a combo of your favorite juice, milk, and water or all water depending on how much sweetness you are after.

Try out some of these combos to get your brain working before you come up with your own shit: tropical fruits like mangoes and pineapples with some coconut milk and water; blueberries or blackberries with almond milk; or do all bananas and sub in peanut butter for $\frac{1}{4}$ cup of the liquids and do the rest with almond milk and water. If it sounds good enough to eat together, then trust that shit will be dope to drink, too.

FRUIT SALAD SMOOTHIE

You could also make this a parfait to crank up the fiber and fullness factor: Sprinkle a layer of ground flaxseeds and rolled oats for every cup of smoothie you pour in the glass. Eat with a spoon or grab a big-ass straw.

MAKES 1 SMOOTHIE

- 2 cups fresh spinach
- 5 pieces frozen bananas, each about 1½ inches long (roughly 1½ bananas)
- 1 cup tap or coconut water
- ½ cup orange juice
- ½ rounded cup frozen strawberries
- ¼ cup frozen blueberries

Throw all that in a blender and let it do its thing. Taste and add more of whatever you want. If you want it thicker, add more banana. This is obviously the kind of thing you eat right away so slam it down as soon as it's ready.

EVEN HEARTLESS ROBOTS
LOVE SMOOTHIES

short order shit

SALADS, SAMMIES, AND MINI MEALS

SPICED CHICKPEA WRAPS WITH TAHINI DRESSING

This captures the smoky flavor of a falafel without all the fucking work.

MAKES 4 BIG WRAPS

TAHINI DRESSING

¼ cup tahini*
3 tablespoons warm water
1½ tablespoons lemon juice
1 tablespoon rice vinegar
1 tablespoon olive oil
1 teaspoon soy sauce or tamari
2 cloves garlic, minced

SPICED CHICKPEAS

1 tablespoon olive oil
3 cups cooked chickpeas**
2 tablespoons lemon juice
1 teaspoon maple syrup
1 teaspoon soy sauce or tamari
2 teaspoons smoked paprika
2 teaspoons ground cumin
1 teaspoon garlic powder
¼ to ½ teaspoon cayenne pepper

4 large wraps or flour tortillas
Spinach
Cucumber sticks
Carrot sticks

1 To make the dressing, mix all that shit together in a small glass until it is smooth and creamy. Set it in the fridge.

2 Now get the chickpeas going. Heat up the olive oil in a large skillet or wok over medium-high heat. Add the chickpeas and fry them until they start to turn gold and pop around a bit. You'll see what the fuck we mean. This will take 3 to 5 minutes. In a small glass, mix together the lemon juice, maple syrup, and soy sauce. When the chickpeas are lookin' right, pour the lemon juice mixture over them and stir. Let that shit evaporate for about 30 seconds and then add all the spices. Stir and let them all fry together for another 30 seconds and then turn off the heat.

3 Serve these spiced sons of bitches in a wrap with some spinach leaves and thinly sliced carrot and cucumber sticks. Drizzle some dressing over it and wrap that shit up.

* *This is like peanut butter but made out of sesame seeds. It will be near the nut butters or falafel mix at the store.*

** *Two 15-ounce cans if you aren't simmering that shit yourself*

HOW TO BUILD A SALAD (AKA "PLANT NACHOS")

We've fucking had it with all this salad shaming. You've probably had some bland-ass salads that wouldn't satisfy a rabbit. Done right, salads are delicious and filling as all hell. It's just a big bowl of plant nachos and we're all about that. Here is a basic guide to building a salad with whatever random shit you have in your kitchen.

1. **THE BASE:** No matter where the fuck you're taking this dish, you need to start off with some greens. This can be spinach, arugula, red leaf, a bag of mixed greens, romaine, kale, cabbage, or whatever you find at the store. Your bowl. Your rules. Generally, the darker the green, the healthier the green, but mixing dark leafy greens in with cheaper lettuces like green leaf will help you stretch your dollars but still mix up your vitamins. The leafy greens base should be about 60 percent of your salad bowl. (Just know that iceberg lettuce is a no-go. Yeah, it is the cheapest thing on the shelf but it's a nutritional nonstarter.) Also, don't always chop the greens the same way. That route is tired as hell. Add some variety by shredding some heartier greens like kale, cutting some crispy lettuces like romaine into thick ribbons, and leaving some leaves like arugula or chicory whole in the same salad to keep shit interesting.

2. **THE ADD-INS:** You always want to throw in a bunch of random veggies. A just-lettuce salad is some sad shit that should only be done the day before your paycheck hits. Add chopped-up vegetables like carrots, cucumbers, bell peppers, tomatoes, broccoli, or fruit like apples, pears, whatever the fuck you like. Add leftover roasted vegetables and potatoes while you're at it. Cooked beans and grains are great here, too. All these extras bring a shitload of vitamins and minerals to your dish while adding even more fiber to keep you full and regular as fuck. These add-ins should count for about 35 percent of your bowl.

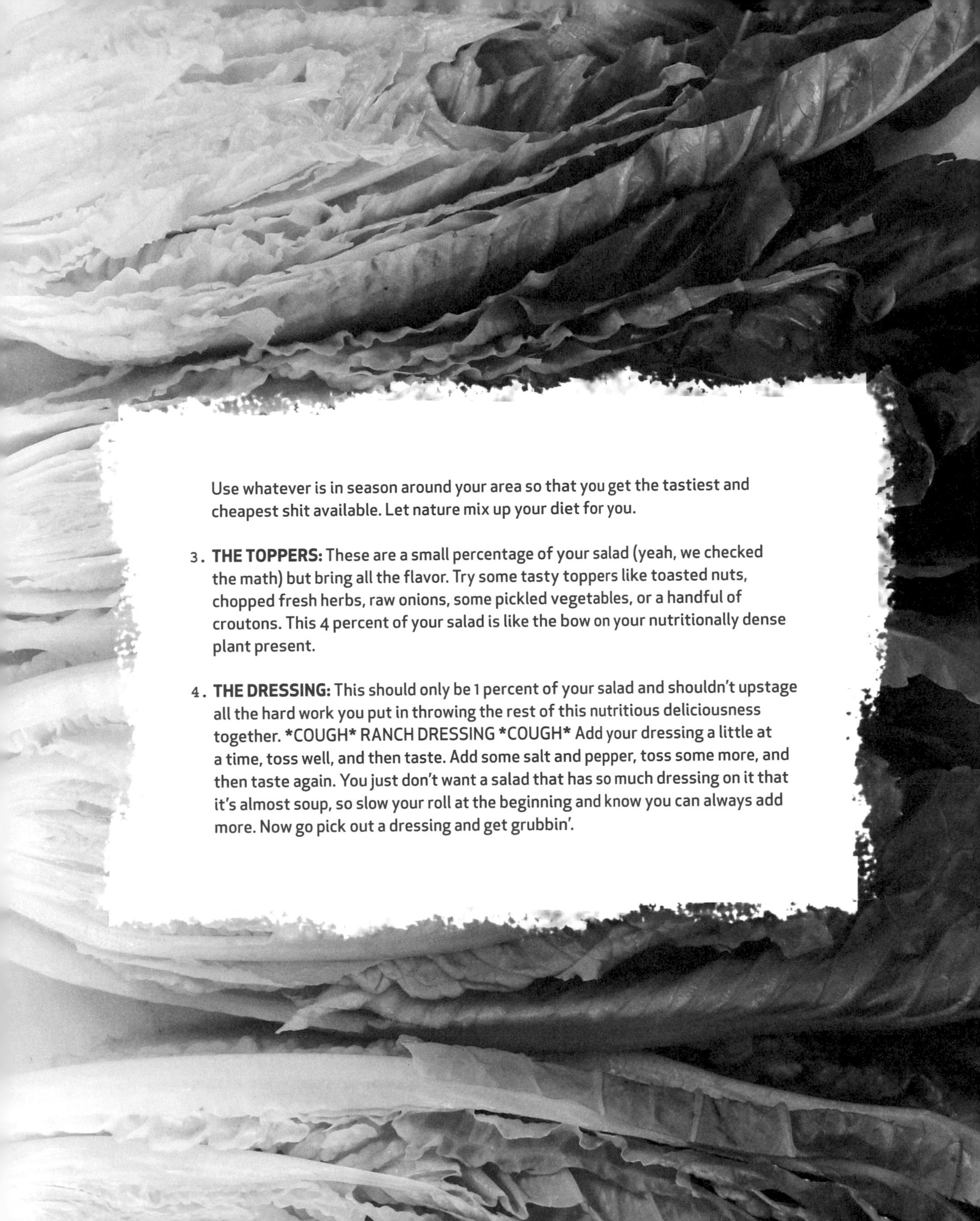

Use whatever is in season around your area so that you get the tastiest and cheapest shit available. Let nature mix up your diet for you.

3. **THE TOPPERS:** These are a small percentage of your salad (yeah, we checked the math) but bring all the flavor. Try some tasty toppers like toasted nuts, chopped fresh herbs, raw onions, some pickled vegetables, or a handful of croutons. This 4 percent of your salad is like the bow on your nutritionally dense plant present.

4. **THE DRESSING:** This should only be 1 percent of your salad and shouldn't upstage all the hard work you put in throwing the rest of this nutritious deliciousness together. *COUGH* RANCH DRESSING *COUGH* Add your dressing a little at a time, toss well, and then taste. Add some salt and pepper, toss some more, and then taste again. You just don't want a salad that has so much dressing on it that it's almost soup, so slow your roll at the beginning and know you can always add more. Now go pick out a dressing and get grubbin'.

DRESS THAT FUCKER UP

Keep a bottle of these bastards in the fridge ready to go and you can have a salad on your table in minutes any night of the week. Each recipe makes around 1 cup of dressing, which is enough for salads all week, unless you're a maniac with dressing distribution. These will separate while you store them, so just shake the shit out of them before you use 'em. They will keep for at least 2 weeks in the fridge.

<<< **TAHINI DRESSING** **(PAGE 32)** Great on all kinds of salads, goes really well with cilantro and basil, and is tasty as hell over some noodles.

ROASTED CARROT AND >>> **CUMIN DRESSING** (opposite) This one's pretty thick but it's really fucking tasty on a simple salad with red onion and cilantro. Hell, it's good on almost anything.

TOASTED SESAME DRESSING

½ cup rice vinegar
1 tablespoon citrus juice*
½ teaspoon soy sauce or tamari
2 tablespoons toasted sesame oil
3 tablespoons olive oil

Pour all the ingredients into a jar and shake that shit up. Taste and add more of whatever-thefuck you think it needs.

** Orange, lime, or lemon works best.*

BASIC THUG KITCHEN VINAIGRETTE

<<<

2 tablespoons diced shallot or sweet onion*
1½ teaspoons Dijon mustard**
¼ cup red wine vinegar
¼ cup rice vinegar
¼ cup olive oil

Pour all this shit together in a jar and shake the fuck out of it. Taste and add more of whatever-thefuck you think it needs. You can switch out the vinegars with what you like to find your favorite combo. If you want to mix it up even more, add 1 teaspoon of your favorite dried herb or herb blend and shake that shit in.

** You can sub in 2 cloves of garlic instead.*

*** This brings the whole dressing together. Trust.*

ROASTED CARROT AND CUMIN DRESSING

3 medium carrots
1 teaspoon olive oil
¼ teaspoon ground cumin
Pinch of salt
⅓ cup white wine vinegar*
¼ cup water
2 tablespoons orange juice
2 tablespoons olive oil

1 Heat up your oven to 375°F. Chop up your carrots into chunks no bigger than ½ inch. Toss them together with the oil, cumin, and salt. Roast them in a small pan, covered, until the carrots are tender, 30 to 40 minutes.

2 Let the carrots cool for a minute then add them to a food processor with the rest of your shit. Blend it until it's smooth. This could take as long as 3 minutes.

** Rice vinegar works, too.*

DON'T FIGHT YOUR
CROUTON
CRAVING
JUSTIFY THAT
SHIT WITH A
SALAD

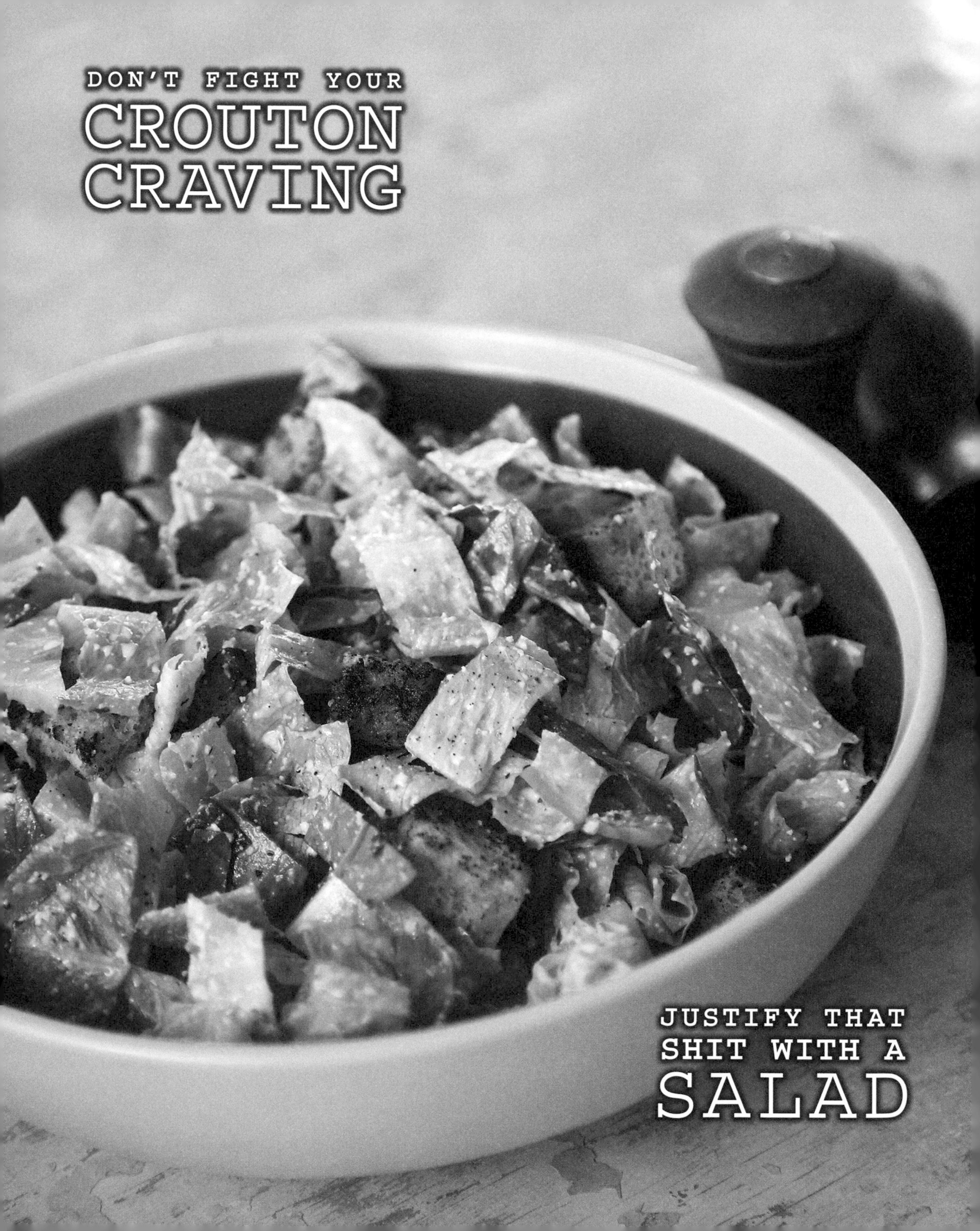

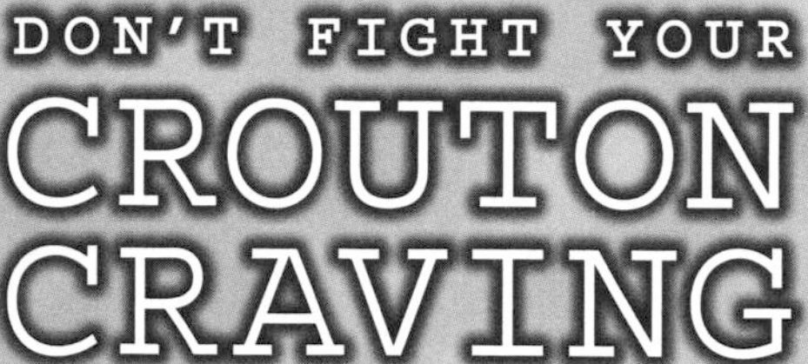

ALMOND CAESAR SALAD WITH HOMEMADE CROUTONS

That empty spot on your plate where a salad should be? Fill it with this and then send your thank-you cards to us.

MAKES ENOUGH FOR 4

⅓ cup sliced or slivered almonds
⅓ cup hot water
1 to 2 cloves garlic
¼ cup olive oil
2 tablespoons lemon juice
1 teaspoon Dijon mustard
1 teaspoon rice vinegar
1 tablespoon capers*
1 head of your favorite lettuce, chopped up
A handful of Homemade Croutons (recipe follows)

1 Put the almonds in a glass with the hot water and let those fuckers soak for about 15 minutes. Chop up the garlic. When the almonds start feeling sorta soft, throw them in a food processor or blender with the water they soaked in, the garlic, olive oil, lemon juice, mustard, and vinegar. Blend it all up until there are no more large almond pieces and it starts to look creamy. You know what the fuck Caesar dressing should look like, come on. Add the capers and run it again for another 5 seconds just so they get chopped up. Chill until you are ready to eat.

2 Serve a couple tablespoons of the dressing over your favorite lettuce with homemade croutons because you know how to live.

** These pickled motherfuckers are near the olives at the store. They sound all fancy, but 1 jar will last you forever and class up your fridge. Throw them in the House Marinara (page 148) with some olives and red pepper flakes and you got yourself a puttanesca, you crazy motherfucker.*

HOMEMADE CROUTONS

MAKES ENOUGH FOR 4 SIDE SALADS

½ loaf day-old bread (enough to make 5 cups of cubes)
3 tablespoons olive oil
1½ tablespoons lemon juice
1½ teaspoons garlic powder
1 teaspoon dried thyme
¼ teaspoon paprika
¼ teaspoon salt

1 Crank your oven to 400°F.

2 Cut up the bread into bite-size cubes. You should get around 5 cups. In a big bowl, combine the rest of the ingredients and mix. Add the bread pieces and mix that fucker up to make sure all the pieces get some love. Pour that out evenly onto a baking sheet and bake for 20 minutes, stirring halfway through to make sure that shit doesn't burn. Serve right away or keep them in an airtight container in the fridge.

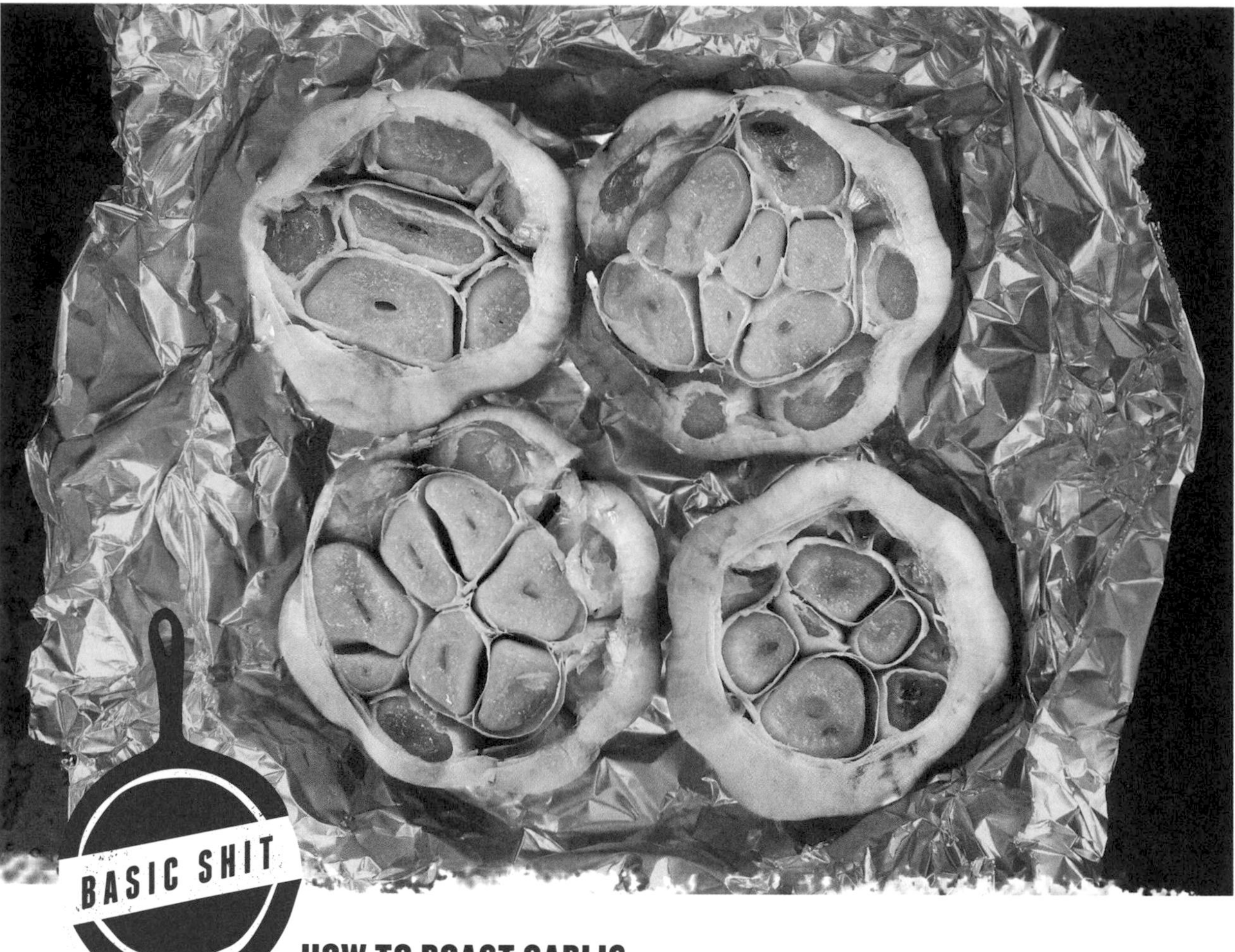

HOW TO ROAST GARLIC

Roasted garlic adds a nice buttery sweetness to just about anything like pasta sauce, salads, and dips and it's easy as hell to make. Stay away from any restaurant that charges extra for this; that's some roasted robbery.

1. **Heat your oven to 400°F.**
2. **Pull off all the extra layers of paper around the bulb of garlic. You want that son of a bitch to stay in one piece, but it doesn't need all that skin holding it back.**
3. **Slice the top ¼ inch right off the bulb of garlic to expose the tips of its innards. Yeah, the motherfucking innards.**
4. **Wrap the whole thing up in foil and drizzle ½ teaspoon olive oil over the top before you close it up. Roast in the oven until the cloves look all golden and smell goddamn delicious, about 40 minutes.**
5. **Let it cool for a bit and then squeeze out as many cloves as you need. It will keep for at least 2 weeks in the fridge.**

DAYS A WEEK
PAPAYA 79¢ LB
TOMATE BOLA $.69 LB
TEXAS ORANGE 79¢ LB
TOMATE ROMA 69¢
YUCA $.99 LB
JICAMA 39
PLATANO MADURO $.79 LB
WHITE ONION CEBOLLA BLANCA .89¢ LB
CEBOLLA AMARILLA 69¢ LB
RED ONION

MOROCCAN SPICED COUSCOUS

Couscous? Oranges? Cinnamon? In a savory dish? Go on, try that shit. We fucking dare you.

MAKES ENOUGH FOR 2 TO 4 AS A SIDE

- 1½ cups couscous
- ¼ teaspoon salt
- ½ teaspoon ground cinnamon
- ½ teaspoon paprika
- ⅛ teaspoon ground cumin
- 1½ cups boiling water
- 1½ tablespoons olive oil
- 2½ tablespoons rice vinegar
- 2 to 3 cups spinach*
- 1 cup chopped orange segments**

1 Mix the couscous, salt, and spices in a medium saucepot with a tight-fitting lid. Add the boiling water to the couscous mix without splashing it around and burning the fuck out of your hand. Stir everything up and quickly put on the lid. Let it rest for at least 8 minutes. The couscous should absorb all the water while you wait and it should be tender when you take off the lid. Easy shit.

2 While your ass is waiting, mix together the olive oil and rice vinegar in a small glass. Chop up the spinach into thick ribbons.

3 When the couscous is ready, stir it around with a fork to fluff it up, add the dressing to it, and stir it up some more until it is mixed. Gently fold in the orange pieces and spinach. Season to your fucking taste . Serve cold or at room temperature.

** Shredded kale would be cool too.*

*** It takes about 5 small oranges to get there but if you have bigger oranges it should only take 1 or 2.*

ROASTED BROCCOLI AND MILLET PILAF

Millet might look like birdseed, but it packs a shitton of heart-healthy magnesium and it's cheap as hell. Try something new and give your heart a chance to get broken instead of attacked.

MAKES ENOUGH FOR 4 AS A SIDE

1 crown broccoli
1 teaspoon plus 1 tablespoon olive oil
1 cup uncooked millet*
2 cups water
Salt and ground pepper
5 cloves roasted garlic**
1 tablespoon lemon juice

1 Crank your oven to 400°F. Grab a rimmed baking sheet.

2 Cut the broccoli into chunks no bigger than your thumb. Toss the broccoli with 1 teaspoon of the oil, pour it in one layer on the baking sheet, and roast the broccoli until it looks a little charred, about 20 minutes.

3 While the broccoli is roasting, make the millet. Grab a medium saucepan and throw it over a medium heat, no oil needed. Add the millet and stir it around until it smells toasted or until you're over it, about 2 minutes. This helps the millet taste nuttier and more awesome, but if you don't give a damn about depth of flavor, you could just move the fuck on. Pour in the water and a pinch of salt and bring this all to a boil. Now turn down the heat so that the pot is at a simmer, cover it, and let it go until the millet is tender, about 25 minutes.

4 You should have a couple minutes to make the sauce before all that finishes up. Grab a glass and smash the roasted garlic cloves around in the bottom of it until a paste forms. Add the lemon juice, remaining 1 tablespoon olive oil, and ¼ teaspoon salt until it looks like a really thick sauce/paste hybrid. Done.

5 When the millet is ready, pour it into a large bowl and add the roasted garlic sauce. Stir everything around really well and then fold in the broccoli. Taste and add more salt, pepper, or lemon juice to suit your tastes. Serve this simple side dish warm or at room temperature.

* *WTF? See page xxiii.*

** *Don't know how to roast garlic? Turn to page 40 and get schooled.*

LEMON-MINT QUINOA

Show people you know that mint isn't just a flavor of gum.

MAKES ENOUGH FOR 4 AS A SIDE

1 teaspoon plus 2 tablespoons olive oil
1½ cups quinoa*
2¾ cups water
¼ teaspoon salt
½ teaspoon grated lemon zest**
2 tablespoons lemon juice
1½ tablespoons rice vinegar
⅓ cup chopped fresh mint
2 tablespoons minced green onions
½ cup slivered almonds, toasted (optional)***

1 Grab a medium saucepan with a lid and heat 1 teaspoon of the oil over medium heat. Add the quinoa and sauté it around until it starts to smell a little nutty, about 2 minutes. Add the water and salt and bring it to a boil. Cover, reduce the heat, and let that simmer until the quinoa is tender, 15 to 18 minutes. If the quinoa is ready but there is water left at the bottom, just drain it in your mesh strainer, return it to the pot, and cover it with a towel while you get your other shit in order.

2 Mix together the lemon zest, lemon juice, vinegar, and remaining 2 tablespoons olive oil in a small glass. After the quinoa has cooled for a couple of minutes, add the lemon dressing, mint, and green onions to it. Toss well and fold in the almonds. Taste to see if you want more salt, mint, or whatthefuckever. Serve at room temperature or cold.

* *Rinse it under some cool water to make sure it isn't bitter as fuck when you cook it.*

** *Just use the smallest side on your box grater to grate the zest. You don't need any fancy equipment.*

*** *The almonds are optional but add a fucking crunch you won't regret.*

ROASTED POTATO SALAD WITH FRESH HERBS

Level up your next potluck with this spud salad. The fresh herbs will make you forget all about that nasty mayo-covered crap you are used to choking down at picnics.

MAKES ENOUGH FOR 4 AS A SIDE

- 1 pound small white or yellow potatoes, unpeeled
- 1 tablespoon olive oil
- ½ teaspoon smoked paprika (optional)*
- ¼ teaspoon salt

FRESH HERB SAUCE

- ½ cup diced fresh parsley
- ½ cup sliced green onions
- 1 clove garlic, minced
- 2 tablespoons olive oil
- 2 tablespoons red wine vinegar
- 1 tablespoon water
- 1 teaspoon lemon juice

1 Crank your oven to 400°F.

2 Slice the potatoes in half lengthwise. If for some reason your little potatoes are not bite-size, then cut those fuckers into quarters instead and throw them in a bowl. Toss the potatoes with the olive oil, paprika, and salt until they all look covered. Pour them onto a rimmed baking sheet in a single layer and roast the hell outta them for 25 minutes, flipping them over halfway through.

3 While the potatoes are roasting, make that herb sauce. You can throw all the ingredients into a food processor and let it rip until everything is minced and mixed together, or you could just mince and mix by hand if you don't want to create another dirty dish.

4 When the potatoes are tender, let them cool for about 10 minutes. Pour them into a large bowl and cover them with the herb sauce, making sure every spud gets some love. Taste and add some salt and pepper until it's howeverthefuck you like it. Stick it in the fridge for at least 1 hour so that the potatoes can absorb all that flavor and the garlic can mellow the fuck out. Serve cold or at room temperature.

* *Optional but dope*

DROPPING KNOWLEDGE

KNIFE SKILLS

We thought we'd throw in a picture to show you exactly what the fuck we're talking about when we ask you to cut shit up. You might not give a damn, but the size of your veggies can make or break a meal. Different-size cuts change cooking times, the texture of your food, and how it all tastes. Think it through: Giant chunks of onion are a whole different thing from some tiny diced-up motherfuckers when you're making marinara. Try to follow what we suggest in each recipe so that your food turns out as dope as possible and be sure to keep your knife sharp as fuck.

FLORETS / TINY TREES
CUBES
HALF MOONS
PLANKS
THICK STRIPS
THIN STRIPS/MATCHSTICKS
SMALL CHOP/DICE
MINCE

EL GUAPO FINALLY MET HIS MATCH

A BATTLE OF THE FITTEST

BRAISED WINTER CABBAGE AND POTATOES

This side dish is some simple shit. Chop. Pour. Roast. Flip. Done. It's great in the middle of winter when all the other veggies in the store are looking sad. GIVE CABBAGE A CHANCE.

MAKES ENOUGH FOR 4 TO 6 AS A SIDE

1 small head of green cabbage (about 1 pound)
½ yellow onion
3 carrots
1 cup vegetable broth
2 tablespoons olive oil
½ pound small white or golden potatoes
3 cloves garlic, minced
1 tablespoon chopped fresh rosemary
Salt and ground pepper
1 tablespoon lemon juice

1 Heat your oven to 350°F.

2 Chop the cabbage in half and slice into wedges no thicker than 2 inches. If it has an extra thick core, chop that fucker right out. Roughly chop the onion and carrots. Big chunks are fine because they are going to have time to cook all the way through.

3 Grab a 9 x 13-inch baking dish and lay the cabbage pieces all down in one layer. Throw the chopped onion and carrots all around them and then pour in the broth and oil. Cover with foil and stick in the oven for 40 minutes.

4 While that cabbage business is braising, slice the small potatoes in half. You want chunks about the size of the head of a soup spoon. When 40 minutes have gone by, take the cabbage out of the oven and turn the wedges over. Next, add the potatoes all over those motherfuckers and sprinkle in the garlic, rosemary, and ¼ teaspoon salt. Stir the potatoes around so that they kinda get some of the remaining broth on them, but don't spend a lot of time on this. It's not worth a bunch of trouble. Cover that fucker back up and let it bake for 40 more minutes, then take off the foil, and let it go for 10 more minutes.

5 When all that time has passed, take that heavy-ass dish out of the oven, drizzle the lemon juice over it, and add salt and pepper to taste. Serve warm. Some vinegary hot sauce on those potatoes wouldn't be the worst idea.

ROASTED BEET AND QUINOA SALAD

When beets are bad, they are really fucking gross. But roasted, these motherfuckers get sweet and delicious. Trust.

MAKES ENOUGH FOR 4 AS A SIDE

DRESSING

1 shallot or small onion, diced (about 2 tablespoons)
1 teaspoon Dijon mustard
3 tablespoons white wine, balsamic, or champagne vinegar
¼ cup olive oil

SALAD

3 medium beets, peeled and chopped into small chunks (about 1½ cups)
1 teaspoon of whatever vinegar you used for the dressing
2 teaspoons olive oil
Salt and ground pepper
2 cups water
1 cup quinoa, rinsed
1 cup kale, stems removed, sliced into thin strips
¼ cup diced fresh herbs*

1 Crank your oven to 400°F. Grab a rimmed baking sheet and have it on standby.

2 Make the dressing: Pour all the ingredients together in a jar and shake that shit up.

3 For the salad: In a medium bowl, toss the beets together with the vinegar, olive oil, and a pinch of salt. Your hands might get kinda red and bloody looking from the beets. Don't worry about that shit; it will wash off, so quit complaining. Pour the mixture onto the baking sheet and roast for 20 minutes, stirring the beets halfway through.

4 While the beets roast up, bring the water to a boil in a medium pot. Add the quinoa. Once that shit starts boiling again, cover, and adjust the heat to low. Cook the quinoa at a slow simmer until it is tender, about 15 minutes. Just taste it and you'll figure that shit out. Drain any extra water that remains in the pot and scoop the quinoa into a medium bowl. Fold the kale into the hot quinoa and then add the dressing. Add the fresh herb of your choice and mix well.

5 When the beets are done, fold those ruby red bitches right in to the quinoa. Add salt and pepper to taste. Serve this salad at room temperature or refrigerate until cold.

** Dill, basil, and parsley all work well here. Use whichever of those you've got hanging out in the fridge.*

VIETNAMESE RICE NOODLE SALAD

When it's hot as hell out and you need a refreshing lunch, make this a meal by topping it with some Ginger-Sesame Baked Tofu (page 77) and see what the fuck is up.

MAKES ENOUGH FOR 4 AS MAIN, 6 AS A SIDE

- 1 package (6.75 ounces) maifun or thin rice noodles
- ½ head of lettuce, chopped*
- 2 medium carrots, cut into matchsticks
- 1 cucumber, peeled and cut into matchsticks
- 1 cup thinly sliced fresh mint leaves
- 1 cup thinly sliced fresh basil leaves
- 1 cup chopped cilantro leaves
- 1 cup sliced green onions
- Toasted Sesame Dressing (page 37), with 1 clove minced garlic added for an extra special something
- ½ cup salted, roasted peanuts, finely chopped
- Lime wedges, for serving

1 Cook the noodles according to package directions. When they are done, drain the noodles and run them under cold water until they are cool to the touch. Set aside.

2 While all that is going down, you should get all your veggies and herbs ready and make your dressing.

3 To serve, pile a large mound of noodles in the center of each plate. Arrange the lettuce, veggies, and herbs around the mound while leaving a good amount of the noodles exposed. Drizzle the dressing on both the noodles and lightly around the vegetables and herbs, then sprinkle the peanuts all over that delicious bitch. Serve with lime wedges.

* *Red leaf, butter, whatever. Just a soft, leafy lettuce. Don't overthink it.*

FORGET THE
FIVE-DOLLAR
FAKE OUT
EAT A REAL
FUCKING
SANDWICH

SMOKED ALMOND AND CHICKPEA SALAD SAMMIES

You don't even know about this sandwich. Like goddamn, we can't even . . . just fucking make it. Trust.

MAKES 4 TO 6 SANDWICHES DEPENDING ON HOWEVER FUCKING HIGH YOU STACK YOUR SAMMIE

QUICK SMOKED ALMONDS*

- 2½ teaspoons liquid smoke**
- ½ teaspoon olive oil
- 1 teaspoon soy sauce, tamari, or Bragg's*
- 1 teaspoon maple syrup or other liquid sweetener
- 2 teaspoons nutritional yeast**
- 1 teaspoon smoked paprika
- 1 teaspoon garlic powder
- ¾ cup raw almonds

SAMMIES

- 3 cups cooked chickpeas***
- 1 avocado
- 3 tablespoons lemon juice****
- ¾ cup chopped red onion (about ½ medium onion)
- ⅓ cup chopped fresh dill
- ⅓ cup chopped celery (about 2 ribs)
- 1 to 2 teaspoons of your favorite hot sauce
- ½ teaspoon salt
- Ground pepper to taste
- 8 to 12 slices bread, toasted
- Dijon mustard, lettuce, and tomato

1 Heat your oven to 350°F. Lightly grease a baking sheet.

2 To make the almonds: Mix together all the liquid ingredients in a small bowl and combine the nutritional yeast, paprika, and garlic powder in a separate bowl. Grab the almonds, add them to the liquid bowl, and stir that together to make sure all the almonds are covered. Scoop out the almonds, add them to the bowl with all the dry seasonings, and stir that shit around until they are covered. When they look all seasoned, scoop them out and lay them on the baking sheet. Toast them in the oven for 10 minutes, stir them around, and then put them back in the oven for 5 more minutes. Take them out and let those sons of bitches cool.

3 While all that shit is happening, add the chickpeas, avocado, and lemon juice to a big bowl and mash the fuck out of them. Some chunks are fine, whatever you like. Fold in the onion, dill, celery, hot sauce, salt, and pepper, then mix it all together.

4 Once the almonds have cooled, chop them up and add them to the bowl.

5 Serve up this badass filling on some toasted bread with Dijon mustard, lettuce, and tomato. This is best enjoyed the day it's made; it keeps fine in the fridge but you might lose some of that crunch.

* *You can buy smoked almonds at the store if you are feeling lazy.*

** *WTF? See page 10.*

*** *Or two 15-ounce cans*

**** *About 1 lemon*

DROPPING KNOWLEDGE

TOFU VS. TEMPEH

When it comes to eating a plant-based diet, you're going to come across some soy. That's how shit goes. But soy gets a bad rap in places where it is not a traditional food. Fucking haters. Not only is it a low-calorie, low-fat source of protein, the American Cancer Society says that eating soy foods like tofu and tempeh may help lower the risk of many cancers. It is important to know the difference so you know what the fuck you're eating and the best way to cook it. And stop worrying about that estrogen bullshit. Do you only eat meat that comes from male animals? No? Then shut the fuck up.

TOFU is more common and way more hated. Tofu is made from soymilk that has been curdled and made to thicken into bricks. By itself, it can be soft and have no flavor. People who don't know what they are doing serve this protein powerhouse with no fucking seasoning and it sucks. Don't let a bad cook ruin a whole goddamn food group. One cup of tofu has 20 grams of protein, is rich in calcium and iron, and is cholesterol free. You can find it in the fridge packed in water and in aseptic containers near the soy sauce at the store.

TEMPEH sounds like some straight-up hippie nonsense but it's damn delicious. It's a brick made of fermented soybeans. They came up with this motherfucker in Indonesia and it's becoming popular as hell. Because it is fermented, sometimes it might look like it has some mold on it, but just fucking go with it. It is firm and chewy and adds a great texture to whatever the fuck you're cooking. Like tofu, it helps to know what you're doing when you are cooking it, so follow one of the recipes in this book and don't wing it. And if you're keeping score, 1 cup of tempeh has 30 goddamn grams of protein in it. You can find it in the fridge of a well-stocked grocery store and on the Internet.

SAVORY TEMPEH AND CARROT SANDWICHES

Don't be surprised if this solid sandwich becomes part of your lunch rotation. The smoky, marinated carrots add a dope crunch that will shame other sandwiches.

MAKES 4 REGULAR-SIZE SANDWICHES

8 ounces tempeh

2 medium carrots

SMOKY MARINADE

1 cup vegetable broth or water

¼ cup soy sauce or tamari

2 tablespoons lemon juice

1½ tablespoons liquid smoke*

2 teaspoons maple syrup or other syrupy sweetener

4 cloves garlic, cut into thick slices

½ teaspoon ground cumin

ASSEMBLY

1 tablespoon olive oil

Lettuce, sliced tomato, avocado, red onion, and mustard

4 rolls or 8 slices of bread, toasted

1 Slice the tempeh into planks about ¼ inch thick and 2 inches long. Do the same thing with the carrots so that they are a similar size and shape. No need to fucking measure it out, just eyeball it.

2 Next, make the marinade: Stir everything together in a saucepan over medium-low heat and bring it to a simmer. Add the tempeh and carrots and gently stir them around. They won't all be covered, just fucking make it work the best you can. After everything simmers together for about 30 seconds, turn off the heat and pour it all into a shallow dish like a pie pan or some shit. Cover that up and stick it in the fridge to marinate for at least 4 hours and up to 8. Yeah, plan ahead, you lazy fuck. We told you to read the goddamn recipe first.

3 When you're ready to assemble your sandwiches, fry up your tempeh and carrots: In a large skillet or wok, heat up the oil over medium heat. Lay the tempeh and carrot planks down in one layer and cook them until the tempeh starts to brown, 2 to 3 minutes on each side. The carrots can cook a little faster so keep an eye on that shit. When it starts to look a little dry in there, or the tempeh feels like it might be sticking, just add a couple spoonfuls of the marinade.

4 Once the tempeh is browned on both sides, then you are ready to make a badass sandwich. Pile lettuce, tomato, avocado, and red onions onto your favorite toasted bread with a little mustard. Add a layer of carrot planks and then the tempeh, close that motherfucker up, and go to town. If you need more help with how to assemble a sandwich, check around on the Internet, then go cry yourself to sleep.

** WTF? See page 10.*

GINGER-MUSHROOM SUMMER ROLLS

These are like sexy, chilled, see-through burritos. Pass them around at a party and watch everyone be like "Daaammn."

MAKES 10 TO 12 ROLLS THAT WILL HAVE PEOPLE TALKING FOR WEEKS

FILLING

- 8 ounces mushrooms*
- 3 cloves garlic
- ½ teaspoon neutral-tasting oil like grapeseed
- 1½ teaspoons soy sauce or tamari
- ⅓ cup minced green onions
- 2 tablespoons minced fresh ginger
- ½ teaspoon toasted sesame oil

SWEET AND SOUR DIPPING SAUCE (OPTIONAL)

- ½ cup rice vinegar
- 2 tablespoons sugar
- 2 to 3 teaspoons chili-garlic paste**
- 1 teaspoon lime juice
- ¼ cup chopped peanuts

ROLLS

- 6 lettuce leaves
- 1 cucumber
- 1 carrot
- 1 cup fresh herbs***
- 1 pack of large spring roll wrappers/rice paper wrappers****

1 Trim and slice the mushrooms into strips no thicker than your finger and mince the garlic. Heat up the neutral oil in a wok or skillet over medium heat. Add the mushrooms and sauté until they start releasing a bunch of liquid, 1 to 2 minutes. Add the soy sauce, green onions, ginger, and garlic and cook until most of that liquid shit evaporates, about 2 more minutes. Add the toasted sesame oil, stir to combine, and turn off the heat. Put the filling on a plate to cool and take a second to wipe down the wok; you'll be saving yourself clean up time later. You're fucking welcome.

2 If you are making the dipping sauce, do that shit now. Throw the vinegar and sugar into a small saucepot and bring it to a simmer over medium heat. Let that cook for about 4 minutes, stirring occasionally. Stir in the chili paste and lime juice and turn off the heat. Once it cools for a couple minutes, pour that shit into a glass and stick it in the fridge. Hold tight on those peanuts.

3 Now let's chop some fucking veggies. This recipe is pretty flexible when it comes to fillings, so feel free to use what you've got. Just make sure that you have some lettuce, something crunchy (like cucumber and carrots), and at least one herb. Almost anything tastes good in here. Just cut everything up except the lettuce into strips about 2 inches long. Cut the lettuce into thirds.

* *Enoki, shiitake, button, whateverthefuck you find is cool.*

** *You can find this by the soy sauce in the store.*

*** *A combo of cilantro, mint, and basil is so fucking good, but use whichever of those you can find.*

**** *They look like a stack of white paper frisbees. They are usually near the soy sauce at the store and are cheap as fuck.*

(you aren't fucking done . . . go to page 58)

OH SHIT
ARE THOSE
MOTHERFUCKING
SUMMER ROLLS?
YOU'RE
DAMN
RIGHT

4 Now for the real bougie shit. Warm about 3 inches of water in the same wok or skillet you cooked the mushrooms. You want the water hot but not so hot you can't put your hand in it. Like tea temperature or some shit like that. Turn off the heat. Place one spring roll wrapper flat in the water for 10 to 15 seconds until it becomes bendy like a noodle. Let the extra water drip off and lay that translucent son of a bitch down on a plate.

5 Fold the wrapper in half so that it looks like a flat taco, straight edge on the bottom. Lay down a lettuce leaf, about 2 fingers' worth of veggies and herbs, and a scoop of the sautéed mushrooms on the left side of the semicircle wrapper thing you've got going. Fold the wrapper over once, left to right, and then fold the bottom up like a burrito. Continue rolling kinda tightly and press the end flap gently against the roll. If you can make a burrito then you already have this shit on lock. Keep making rolls until you run out of filling.

6 To serve, add the chopped peanuts to the dipping sauce and go to town. Finished rolls will keep in the fridge for about 2 days but if you haven't eaten them by then, you're fucking crazy.

HERBAL HAZE

Fresh herbs, get to know 'em. We call for a lot of dried herbs in this book because they're cheaper and easier to keep on hand for whenever you need to get down in the kitchen. They're great for adding to a dish early in the cooking process because they need time to moisten up and release all their tasty flavors. But if you are looking to kick any meal up a notch, just use fresh herbs. They obviously taste a little fresher and brighter than their dried out bastard brothers and can be a simple way to mix shit up.

In general, dried herbs are more concentrated than fresh, so you'll want to multiply any dried herb measurement by 3 if you sub in the fresh shit. So like 1 teaspoon dried thyme in a recipe would be 3 teaspoons/1 tablespoon fresh thyme leaves. Boom. Also, if your dish looks generally fucked up, just sprinkle on some chopped fresh herbs like parsley, basil, or cilantro at the end and it will look all artisan and shit. Works every time.

BARLEY-STUFFED PEPPERS

Barley is a goddamn delicious grain that looks a lot like rice, but tastes more peppery. It's also full of good shit for you like manganese, dietary fiber, selenium, and niacin. So why the fuck wouldn't you try it?

MAKES 4 STUFFED PEPPERS

- 2 tablespoons olive oil
- ½ onion, chopped
- 2 ribs celery, chopped
- 1 carrot, chopped
- 3 to 4 cloves garlic, minced
- 2 teaspoons dried thyme
- 1½ teaspoons dried oregano
- 1 cup pearled barley
- 1 tomato, chopped (about ½ cup)
- 2 tablespoons sherry vinegar or red wine vinegar
- 2 cups vegetable broth
- ½ teaspoon salt
- ¼ teaspoon ground pepper
- 4 bell peppers, whatever color you find is cool
- 1½ cups cooked kidney or white beans*
- ¼ cup chopped fresh parsley

1 In a medium pot, heat the oil over medium heat. Add the onion and cook until it starts turning golden, about 3 minutes. Add the celery, carrot, garlic, thyme, and oregano and cook for another 2 minutes. Throw in the barley, tomato, and vinegar and stir. Add the broth, salt, and pepper and let it come to a low simmer. Cook, uncovered, until all the broth is absorbed and the barley is tender, about 15 minutes.

2 While the barley is simmering, heat your oven to 375°F. Cut the tops off the bell peppers and scrape out any seeds. Place them in an oiled pie plate or loaf pan, something where their asses won't be sliding around once they're stuffed.

3 When the barley is done, fold in the beans and turn off the heat. (This filling can even be made a day or two ahead of time, no fucking problem.) Fill the bell peppers up to the top with the filling, cover them tightly with foil, and bake until the peppers are tender, 45 minutes to 1 hour. Let them rest for 5 minutes after coming out of the oven, 'cause those fuckers are hot. Top with the parsley and serve.

* *Or one 15-ounce can*

GRILLED EGGPLANT WITH SOBA NOODLES

Perfect for the middle of summer when basil and eggplant price have hit rock-bottom and you've spent all of your fucking money on a new fan.

MAKES ENOUGH FOR 4 PEOPLE OR JUST 1 IF YOU WANT TO SAVE THIS STUFF FOR LUNCH ALL WEEK.

EGGPLANT AND MARINADE

½ cup rice vinegar

¼ cup water

¼ cup tamari or soy sauce

2 tablespoons toasted sesame oil

1 tablespoon agave syrup or other liquid sweetener

2 cloves garlic, minced

1 medium eggplant (about 1 pound)

NOODLES

8 ounces soba noodles*

1 tablespoon toasted sesame oil

1 tablespoon rice vinegar

3 tablespoons water

½ cup fresh basil cut into thin ribbons

1½ tablespoons sesame seeds

1 Mix up everything for the marinade in a glass. Slice the eggplant crosswise into ¼-inch rounds. Place the eggplant in a large pan of some kind and pour the marinade over that shit. Let the eggplant marinate for at least 15 minutes or up to 1 hour if you've got the fucking time.

2 While the eggplant marinates, cook the soba noodles according to the package directions. Drain the noodles and rinse them with cool water so that they aren't still cooking. Place them in a large bowl and add the toasted sesame oil and rice vinegar. Stir it all up.

3 Bring your grill or grill pan to a medium heat (around 300° to 350°F). Oil the grill grates. When the eggplant is done marinating, grill the eggplant slices (but don't throw away that marinade) on each side 2 to 3 minutes or until you see some grill marks. If the eggplant begins to look a little dry, take the slices and dip them in or brush them with the remaining marinade and continuing cooking them until done. Eggplant hydration. Boom.

4 When all of the eggplant is done cooking and has cooled slightly, cut it up into ½-inch squares. Mix together ½ cup of the leftover marinade and the 3 tablespoons of water. Pour that mess all over the noodles and mix. Toss in the eggplant and basil and mix again. Top with sesame seeds and serve at room temperature or cold.

* *You can use whole wheat pasta or whatever here, but soba noodles—made of buckwheat flour—taste way fucking better.*

SWEET CORN AND GREEN CHILE BAKED FLAUTAS

If you know what flautas are, then we don't need to sell you on them. If you don't know what flautas are, then grab your lunch box because we're taking your ass to school. Serve them with salsa and guacamole if you're feeling fancy.

MAKES ABOUT 12 FLAUTAS USING STANDARD FLOUR TORTILLAS

Cooking spray
1 teaspoon olive oil
1 cup chopped yellow or white onion (about ½ onion)
2 teaspoons chili powder
¾ teaspoon ground cumin
½ teaspoon salt
4 to 5 cloves garlic, chopped
3 cups cooked pinto beans
1 can (4 ounces) mild green chiles*
Juice of ½ lime
1 cup sweet corn kernels**
12 flour tortillas

** These should be in a tiny can near the salsa in your grocery store. If you can't find them, you can roast 2 poblano peppers following the method for bell peppers on page 161.*

*** This is about 1 cob's worth. That's a fucking ridiculous phrase but whatever. You can use frozen if that's all you can find.*

1 Crank your oven to 400°F. Grab a large baking sheet and coat it with a little cooking spray.

2 Heat up the oil in a large sauté pan over medium heat and throw in the onion. Cook until the onion starts to brown, about 5 minutes. Add the chili powder, cumin, salt, and garlic and cook for another 30 seconds and then turn off the heat.

3 Throw the beans, chiles, and lime juice together in a big-ass bowl. Mash them up using a potato masher or a spoon until a paste forms. It's cool if there are some whole beans left here and there; you don't need to spend the whole goddamn day mashing. Fold in the sautéed onions and corn and stir that motherfucker up. Your filling is ready.

4 Using a griddle, your oven, or the microwave, warm up the tortillas. Grab about 2 heaping tablespoons of the filling and spread that shit in a nice line toward the edge of the left side of one of the tortillas from top to bottom. Then roll that shit up nice and tight from left to right. You could even put a small smear of beans toward the other end of the tortilla to help that fucker stay shut. Place the flauta seam side down on the baking sheet about an inch or two away from its flauta brethren. Make sure the filling got all the way to the ends and then adjust how you distribute the filling the next time. Damn. Keep going until you run out of tortillas or filling.

5 Lightly coat them all with cooking spray and bake for 10 minutes. When you pull them out, the bottoms should be golden—if not, stick them in for another couple minutes. When the bottoms look good, turn them over and bake those bitches until they're golden and crispy on both sides, another 5 to 7 minutes. Serve warm topped with lettuce and salsa if you want to impress some motherfuckers.

FLAUNT YOUR
FLAUTAS

SMOKY BLACK-EYED PEAS WITH ROASTED SWEET POTATOES AND COLLARDS

Nobody is going to be picky when you serve up this tasty-ass plate. A little sweet, a little smoky, but all around goddamn delicious.

MAKES ENOUGH FOR 6

- 1½ cups dried black-eyed peas
- 6 medium to large sweet potatoes
- 2 teaspoons olive oil
- 1 onion, chopped into pea-size pieces
- 3 ribs celery, chopped into pea-size pieces
- ¼ teaspoon salt
- ½ teaspoon ground allspice*
- ½ teaspoon ground nutmeg
- ½ teaspoon paprika
- 2 to 3 cloves garlic, minced
- 3 to 4 chipotle peppers in adobo sauce, chopped into pea-size pieces**
- 3 cups vegetable broth
- 2 or 3 batches Wilted Greens (page 80)

1 Rinse the black-eyed peas and throw out any grit or fucked-up looking peas. Put the peas in a large bowl and cover them with a couple inches of water. Let them soak overnight or for at least 6 hours. After soaking, drain the peas and start fucking cooking.

2 Before you start to cook the peas, crank your oven to 400°F. Grab your sweet potatoes and stab the fuck out of them with a fork in a couple spots. This helps the steam release while they roast and helps you get some of that stabbiness out your system. Put them on a baking sheet and sit them in the oven until you can stick a knife through them without resistance, about 45 minutes.

3 Now back to the black-eyed peas. In a large pot, heat the olive oil over medium heat. Add the onion and sauté that shit until it starts to brown in some places, about 5 minutes. Add the celery and cook until it starts to get a little soft, about 2 minutes. Add the salt and spices and sauté for 30 seconds. Add the garlic and chipotles to the pot and cook for another 30 seconds.

4 Toss the drained black-eyed peas into the pot along with the broth and bring that shit to a simmer. Let it simmer uncovered until the peas are tender. This can take anywhere from 30 minutes to 1 hour depending on how long you soaked your peas and how old they are. If you start running out of liquid before those are ready, add a little more broth or water. If the peas are tender and you've still got too much broth in there, just drain some of that shit off. Not a big fucking deal. Just check the seasoning when you are all done and add more herbs or spices if you think it needs it.

HOW THE FUCK DO
YOU THINK THOSE
PEAS GOT
BLACK
EYES?

5 Make your wilted collard greens right before the sweet potatoes are done roasting.

6 When the sweet potatoes are done, split them open lengthwise and fluff them with a fork. Feel free to add a little unrefined coconut oil and a pinch of salt to spice those sweet fuckers up. Pour at least 1 cup of peas over the potatoes and 2 cups of the greens. Serve right away.

* *This is not a blend of spices—it's a berry with a confusing ass name. It is in a lot of Caribbean food and should be right next to all the spices and shit in your store.*

** *These smoked peppers in sauce are sold in a tiny can and are usually near the salsa and beans. When you chop the chipotles, cut them open and scrape out the seeds. If you prefer it hot, then keep some of the seeds in, but think of your butt hole tomorrow as you make that call.*

rlos

APPLE BAKED BEANS

These beans are dope alongside the White Bean and Red Lentil Burgers (page 170) or in a bowl (page 174) with the Roasted Broccoli and Millet Pilaf (page 43) and Wilted Greens (page 80).

MAKES ENOUGH FOR 6 AS A SIDE

- **1½ cups dried white beans**
- **5 cups water**
- **2 teaspoons olive oil**
- **½ yellow onion, chopped**
- **1 clove garlic, minced**
- **1 teaspoon smoked paprika**
- **1 can (15 ounces) low- or no-salt tomato sauce**
- **1 tablespoon molasses**
- **1 tablespoon apple cider vinegar**
- **2 tablespoons brown sugar**
- **2 teaspoons soy sauce or tamari**
- **1 sprig fresh rosemary***
- **2½ cups vegetable broth**
- **1 medium apple, whatever kind you like to eat, chopped into bite-size cubes**

1 Sift through the beans and pick out any that look all fucked up. Pour them into a big-ass bowl with the water and let them soak overnight.

2 When your beans are all softened, it's time to make some goddamn dinner. Drain the beans. Grab a large pot and heat the oil over medium heat. Throw in the onion and sauté until it begins to brown, about 5 minutes. Add the garlic and smoked paprika and cook for another 30 seconds. Add the drained beans, tomato sauce, molasses, vinegar, brown sugar, soy sauce, and rosemary. Stir it all up and bring it to a simmer, then add the broth. This might look like you are trying to cast a spell or some shit like that, but just go with it.

3 Let all this simmer together until the beans are almost tender. This should take about 1 hour, but it really depends on how old your beans are and how long you soaked them. Once they are almost done, add the apple. Simmer until the apple is tender and the beans are soft, about 30 minutes more. Take out that rosemary sprig and serve.

* *Yeah, the whole fucking branch and everything. The leaves will fall off as you cook, no big deal. Just pull the stick out when the beans are done.*

5-SPICE FRIED RICE WITH SWEET POTATOES

The trick to good fried rice is to use cold, leftover cooked rice. Freshly cooked rice will get all mushy and that shit just won't work. So don't start bitching if you fuck this up—you've been warned. Add in some Dry-Fried Tofu (page 154) to make this a meal.

MAKES ENOUGH FOR 4 AS A SIDE OR YOUR LONELY ASS FOR A COUPLE OF NIGHTS

- 1 medium sweet potato (¾ to 1 pound)
- 2 teaspoons neutral-tasting oil*
- 2 tablespoons water, plus more if needed
- ½ small yellow onion, chopped
- 1 carrot, chopped
- ¼ teaspoon Chinese 5-spice powder**
- 1 to 2 cloves garlic, minced
- 1½ tablespoons soy sauce or tamari
- 1 tablespoon rice vinegar
- 1 teaspoon chili paste or an Asian-style hot sauce like Sriracha
- 4 cups cooked short-grain brown rice that's been chilled for a couple hours
- 1 cup bitter greens,*** chopped up no bigger than a quarter
- ½ cup sliced green onions
- 1 cup frozen green peas, thawed

1 Peel the sweet potato and chop into dice-size cubes.

2 In a large wok or skillet, heat 1 teaspoon of the oil over medium heat. Add the sweet potato and the water and stir-fry the potato, stirring often. If the potato starts to stick, add a little more of the water as needed. Cook until the potato is close to tender and browning on some sides, 5 to 8 minutes. Add the onion and carrot and cook until the onions are translucent, about 3 more minutes. Add the 5-spice powder and garlic, mix well, then remove the vegetables from the pan. Scrape the pan clean cause we aren't fucking done.

3 In a small glass, mix together the soy sauce, vinegar, and chili paste. Heat the wok back up over medium heat and add the remaining 1 teaspoon oil. Throw in the rice and stir-fry until it begins to warm, 3 to 5 minutes. Drizzle the sauce over the rice, mix well, then add the cooked vegetables. Stir-fry for a minute so everything is well mixed. Fold in the greens, green onions, and peas. Turn off the heat and serve immediately.

* *Grapeseed, peanut, or regular sesame oil would be cool.*

** *Most grocery stores carry this shit with the rest of the spices. It's a blend of cloves, star anise, cinnamon, pepper, ginger, and fennel seeds. It's tasty as hell and you should own some. If you can't find it, you can make your own blend or just leave it out and tell your grocer to get their shit together.*

*** *We used watercress, but mustard or arugula are fine if you can't find that weedy looking bastard.*

TAKEOUT CAN'T TOUCH THIS

STOP SERVING THE SAME
OLD SOGGY SADNESS
AND TRY
THIS
SLAWSOME
SIDE DISH

CREAMY PEANUT SLAW

Mixing peanut butter with cabbage might sound kinda fucked, but it's delicious. This side is dope with the Cold Citrus Noodles (page 75), Grilled Eggplant with Soba Noodles (page 61), and/or the Ginger-Mushroom Summer Rolls (page 56). Hell, you can just eat it solo.

MAKES ENOUGH FOR 4 AS A SIDE

PEANUT DRESSING

- 3 tablespoons peanut butter
- 2 tablespoons warm water
- 3 tablespoons rice vinegar
- 2 tablespoons lime juice
- 1 tablespoon minced fresh ginger
- 1½ teaspoons Sriracha or your favorite Asian-style hot sauce
- ½ teaspoon soy sauce or tamari

SLAW

- 3 cups thinly sliced red cabbage
- 3 cups thinly sliced green cabbage
- 1 carrot, cut into thin matchsticks
- ⅓ cup thinly sliced green onions

1 Make the peanut dressing: Mix the peanut butter and warm water together in a medium glass until it's creamy. Add the rest of the dressing ingredients to the sauce and mix that son of a bitch well.

2 In a large bowl, combine all the slaw veggies. Pour the dressing over them and toss it all around until everything is coated. Serve the day it's made.

COCONUT-LIME RICE WITH RED BEANS AND MANGO

This one-pot wonder makes other side dishes step up their game or be forgotten.

MAKES ENOUGH FOR 4 TO 6 AS A SIDE

2 cups short-grain brown rice
2 teaspoons neutral-tasting oil*
1 cup diced shallots or onion**
1½ tablespoons minced fresh ginger
1 cup canned coconut milk***
2½ cups vegetable broth
¼ teaspoon salt
⅛ teaspoon cayenne pepper****
1 mango
1½ cups cooked red beans*****
Grated zest and juice of 1 lime
Chopped cilantro or green onions, for serving

1 Rinse the rice under cool water. Heat up the oil over medium heat in a large soup pot. Add the shallots and sauté until they start to brown in some spots, about 3 minutes. Add the ginger and sauté for 30 seconds until everything smells choice. Add the rice and keep stirring until the rice starts to smell slightly toasted, about 2 minutes. Add the coconut milk, broth, salt, and cayenne pepper and bring to a simmer. Give the pot a quick stir, cover it, and reduce the heat to low. Keep it all at a very gentle simmer and leave it the fuck alone until the rice is tender and has absorbed nearly all the liquid, about 40 minutes. If your rice isn't done by the time you run out of liquid, don't stress that shit; just add a little more broth or water.

2 While the rice is cooking, chop up the mango into bite-size pieces. (Not sure how to chop that fucker up? Turn to page 74 for the how-to. You should get around 1½ cups of flesh from 1 mango.)

3 When the rice is tender, fold in the beans, lime zest, lime juice, and mango. Let this all cook together for another minute or two so that everything is warmed up. Serve warm topped with cilantro or green onions.

* *Grapeseed, peanut, or regular sesame oil work fucking great.*

** *That's about 4 shallots or ½ small onion.*

*** *See Dropping Knowledge, page 74.*

**** *Leave this shit out if you can't stand the heat.*

***** *Or two 15-ounce cans. Also, you can use black or kidney beans here if you can't find red beans.*

HOW TO CUT A MANGO

Mangoes can be confusing as fuck to cut into because they have a giant, oblong-shaped pit in the center that is hard as shit. Follow these steps and stop wondering how the fuck people do it.

1. Run your knife through the mango from top to bottom avoiding that tough pit. Think like you are peeling a huge chunk of flesh off the pit with your knife. Do that on both sides of the mango pit.
2. Then cut a checkerboard pattern into the flesh of the halves, making sure to not cut through the skin. Next, cut all around the edges between the mango flesh and the skin. Where the fuck is this going?
3. Using your thumbs, flip that shit inside out so that all your sweet mango cubes are waiting for you like a hedgehog made of fruit. Scoop them out with a spoon and get to whatever the fuck you are doing.

LITE COCONUT MILK

Lite coconut milk is just regular coconut milk with a bunch of water mixed in, but that shit is the same price. Grab the full-fat can because you can cut that shit with water at home. Get your motherfucking money's worth.

DROPPING KNOWLEDGE

COLD CITRUS NOODLES WITH CUCUMBERS AND CARROTS

These noodles always hit the fucking spot. They're great served on a bed of greens like spinach and topped with the Ginger-Sesame Baked Tofu (page 77) if you're making it a meal.

MAKES ENOUGH FOR 4 AS A SIDE

CITRUS SESAME SAUCE

¼ cup rice vinegar
2 tablespoons water
2 tablespoons orange juice
2 tablespoons toasted sesame oil
1½ tablespoons minced fresh ginger
1 tablespoon soy sauce or tamari
1 tablespoon lemon juice

NOODLES AND VEGGIES

8 ounces soba noodles*
2 small carrots, cut into matchsticks
2 small cucumbers, cut into matchsticks
⅔ cup thinly sliced green onions
1½ tablespoons toasted sesame seeds

1 Mix all the ingredients for the citrus sesame sauce together in a small glass.

2 Cook the noodles according to the package directions, because all that shit is different. When they are done, drain and rinse them with cold water so that they stop cooking and don't get all mushy.

3 While the noodles are cooking, cut up the veggies and green onions.

4 Add the drained noodles, carrots, cucumbers, and sesame sauce to a large bowl and toss to combine. Fold in the green onions and sesame seeds. Serve cold or at room temp.

* *You can use udon, somen, whole wheat pasta, or whatever here, but soba (made from buckwheat) is the go-to if you can find it.*

HOW TO BAKE TOFU

Why is everyone so fucking afraid of tofu? That shit is just misunderstood. Yeah, it can be bland and mushy, but that is because people don't know how the fuck to cook it right and that gives tofu a bad name. It isn't hard; most motherfuckers are just lazy with it. We got this shit figured out, though. Throw it in a flavorful marinade and bake at a high heat, and tofu turns into something worth eating and not just some health food dare. Try it out and see how much better you can be at this tofuckery than everybody else.

1. Grab some extra-firm tofu, drain it, wrap it in some paper towels or a clean dish cloth, put it between two plates, and put some weight on it like a can of beans. This presses out all that water it's packed in and makes room for flavor. This should take about 30 minutes to 1 hour. So you can go grab a nap or something.

2. Next, mix together your marinade in a shallow, rimmed dish like a pie plate—you know, something where all the tofu can marinate in one layer.

3. Cut the tofu into widthwise planks no thicker than ¼ inch. You should get about 12 pieces per brick of tofu. Throw that in the marinade, make sure all the pieces are covered, and let that sit in the fridge for at least 2 hours and up to 8. Stir it around every now and then if you can remember.

4. When you're ready, crank the oven to 450°F. Grease a rimmed baking sheet.

5. Take the tofu out of the marinade (save the marinade) and arrange the planks on the baking sheet. Bake for 15 minutes, flip, and spoon a little more marinade on each piece. Bake for 10 more minutes, flip, and sauce again. Bake for a final 5. The edges should start looking a little burnt. That's the right way to do it, so just calm the fuck down. Let it sit for a couple minutes to firm up and then cut it into whatever shaped pieces you need.

Marinated, baked tofu is great folded into salads, wraps, and pastas where you need some extra protein and regular beans won't cut it.

Tofu Marinades

After choosing a marinade, mix all the ingredients together in a shallow, rimmed dish that will hold the tofu in one layer (see directions opposite).

MAKES ENOUGH FOR 1 BRICK OF TOFU

GINGER-SESAME MARINADE

¼ cup soy sauce or tamari
¼ cup rice vinegar
2 tablespoons lime juice
2 tablespoons brown sugar
1 tablespoon minced fresh ginger
2 teaspoons toasted sesame oil
2 teaspoons Sriracha or similar hot sauce
2 cloves garlic, thickly sliced

SMOKY MAPLE MARINADE

¼ cup soy sauce or tamari
¼ cup vegetable broth or water
2 tablespoons maple syrup
1 tablespoon liquid smoke*
1 tablespoon lemon juice
1 tablespoon tomato paste
1 tablespoon olive oil
2 cloves garlic, thickly sliced

SWEET CITRUS MARINADE

½ cup orange juice
¼ cup soy sauce or tamari
1 tablespoon brown sugar
1 tablespoon minced fresh ginger
1 tablespoon olive oil
2 teaspoons Sriracha or similar hot sauce
2 cloves garlic, thickly sliced

* *WTF? See page 10.*

YELLOW SPLIT PEA AND GREEN ONION LETTUCE WRAPS

Tired of boring ass lettuce wraps? Us, too. Try these crunchy fuckers out and remember why it's fun to eat with your hands.

MAKES 12 TO 14 LETTUCE WRAPS

1½ cups yellow split peas
3 cups water
Salt

DIPPING SAUCE

2 tablespoons soy sauce or tamari
2 tablespoons water
2 tablespoons rice vinegar
1 to 2 teaspoons of your favorite Asian-style hot sauce*
1 teaspoon toasted sesame oil
1 teaspoon of your favorite liquid sweetener**

WRAPS

2 teaspoons neutral-tasting oil
½ cup chopped shallots or yellow onion
2 teaspoons minced fresh ginger
1 cup minced green onions
⅔ cup shredded carrot***
3 tablespoons rice vinegar
1½ teaspoons soy sauce or tamari
1½ teaspoons toasted sesame oil
1 head of lettuce such as romaine or red leaf

1 Rinse the peas well and then throw them in a medium pot with the water and a pinch of salt and bring them to a boil. Reduce the heat and let those sons of bitches simmer until they are tender, 10 to 15 minutes. You can figure that shit out just by tasting them. When the peas are done, drain them and set aside.

2 While the peas are cooking, mix together all the ingredients for the dipping sauce in a small bowl.

3 Grab a big wok or skillet and heat the oil over medium heat. Add the shallots and sauté until they start to turn golden, about 3 minutes. Add the ginger and green onions and let it all cook together for another 30 seconds. Add the split peas and carrots, toss, then add the rice vinegar and soy sauce. Let that simmer together for another 30 seconds while you stir. Add the toasted sesame oil and then turn off the heat.

4 Serve the filling warm or at room temperature with a bunch of lettuce leaves to use as leafy tortillas. Keep the dipping sauce on the side. Looks like a good fucking time.

* *Optional but you really should try new shit.*

** *Agave or maple syrup would do if that's what you've got.*

*** *Use your box grater.*

GIVE PEAS
A FUCKING
CHANCE

WILTED GREENS

Not sure how to cook greens properly? Let's fix that shit. This is the stupid-simple how-to for the don't-know crowd.

MAKES ENOUGH FOR 2 AS A SIDE

- **1 bunch hearty, dark, leathery greens like kale or collards**
- **½ teaspoon olive or grapeseed oil**
- **1 tablespoon water**
- **2 cloves garlic, minced**
- **2 teaspoons lemon juice**
- **1 teaspoon soy sauce or tamari**

1 Remove the tough stems and slice the greens into strips about 1 inch wide and 2 inches long. You should aim for around 6 cups. This might seem like way too many greens, but they'll cook down to fucking nothing. Trust.

2 Grab a big wok or skillet and heat up the oil over medium heat. Add the greens and toss them around until everything has a little oil on it and cook for about 30 seconds.

3 Add the water, garlic, lemon juice, and soy sauce and then keep tossing those greens around so that it all cooks down. This shouldn't take more than a minute and a half. Once all the greens are wilted, turn off the heat and serve.

BAKED SPANISH RICE

Toss this in the oven and forget about that shit until dinnertime.

MAKES ENOUGH FOR 4 TO 6 AS A SIDE OR 8 AS BURRITO FILLING

1 Crank your oven to 375°F. Grab a 9 x 13-inch glass or ceramic baking dish.

2 In a blender or food processor, combine the onion, tomatoes, garlic, jalapeño, and tomato paste and let that shit run until a smoothish-looking sauce is born, about 30 seconds. You should get about 2 cups of sauce. Pour that into a medium saucepan, mix in the broth, and let it come to a simmer over medium heat.

3 While that tomato mixture is heating up, spread the rice over the bottom of the baking dish and drizzle the oil and salt over the top.

4 When the broth mixture is at a gentle simmer, pour it over the rice, stir it up so everything is mixed, then cover tightly with foil and put in the oven. Let this bake for 1 hour. Try to not check on it because every time you do you'll be letting out precious steam and your rice will be undercooked as a motherfucker. Just keep the oven at 375°F and you're all good.

5 After 1 hour, pull out the baking dish and fluff the rice around with a fork so everything is mixed back in. If the rice isn't all the way cooked, add another ¼ cup broth or water, cover, and bake it for another 10 minutes or so. Fold in the corn, peas, lime juice, and cilantro and mix well. Add a pinch more salt if you need it. Serve right away.

* *These can be fresh or thawed frozen stuff; not a fucking deal breaker here.*

½ onion, chopped (about 1 cup)

2 tomatoes, chopped (about 1¼ cups)

3 cloves garlic, minced

1 jalapeño, minced

1 tablespoon tomato paste

2½ cups vegetable broth

2 cups long-grain brown rice

1½ tablespoons olive or grapeseed oil

½ teaspoon salt

1 cup corn kernels*

1 cup green peas*

1 tablespoon lime juice (about ½ lime)

¼ cup chopped fresh cilantro

big ass cup of cozy

SOUPS AND STEWS

LEMONY RED LENTIL SOUP

This isn't that boring brown lentil mush you find in places where food goes to die. We wouldn't do you like that. The spices and lemon makes this some next-level shit that you will actually want to eat.

MAKES ENOUGH FOR 4 AS A MAIN AND 6 AS A SIDE

1 teaspoon olive or coconut oil
½ yellow onion, chopped
1 fist-size russet (baking) potato, peeled and cut into cubes about the size of dice
1 carrot, chopped
2 cloves garlic, minced
1 teaspoon ground coriander*
½ teaspoon ground cumin
¼ teaspoon salt
2 cups red lentils, rinsed
6 cups vegetable broth
½ teaspoon grated lemon zest
1 tablespoon lemon juice
½ cup chopped fresh cilantro (optional)

1 Grab a large soup pot and heat the oil over medium heat. Add the onion and let it sauté for about 3 minutes, until it starts getting all soft and vaguely golden. Yeah, that's right, "vaguely golden," motherfucker. Now add the potato and carrot. Sauté for another 2 minutes and then add the garlic and spices. At this point, your place should start smelling choice. Sauté for another 30 seconds and then add the salt, lentils, and broth.

2 Let the lentils simmer, uncovered, until they're soft and kinda falling apart, 15 to 20 minutes. Stir this every now and then. Add the lemon zest and juice and turn off the heat. Now you can stop if you prefer a chunky lentil soup, or you can blend half of it for a creamy chunky hybrid thing. It's your soup, so own that shit. The blended soup will thicken up if you throw it back on the stove with some low heat for a minute or two, just watch. Magic, bitches.

3 Serve warm, topped with some chopped cilantro if you want.

* *Coriander is a super tasty seed of the cilantro plant, but it doesn't taste a damn thing like cilantro; it's on another level. If you can't find it at the store, just leave it out and use an extra ½ teaspoon cumin.*

HOW TO MAKE VEGETABLE BROTH WITH SCRAPS

A lot of recipes in here call for vegetable broth and we don't want you just relying on that shelf-stable bullshit you get at the store. You can totally make that flavored water yourself from scraps you are leaving behind as you cook. It is as easy as stuffing scraps in a bag and boiling water. Look at your fine ass, saving money and reducing waste.

Keep a gallon bag in your freezer and throw in scrap bits of produce you end up with as you cook. Think ends of onions, carrot peels, celery, garlic, shallots, green onion pieces, and the ends of leeks. Also, toss in any shit you might have overbought and is starting to look not so hot. Mushrooms, bell peppers, fennel, and herbs like parsley, rosemary, and thyme that got dried out or wilted as fuck are great too. Just don't throw in bitter shit like cabbage, broccoli, cauliflower, or Brussels sprouts or anything that is starting to rot or mold. Basically, if you think that the water some vegetable was boiled in might taste good, then try that fucker out. This is the simplest shit there is.

1. **When your bag is really full, it's time to get boiling. You want around 5 cups of scraps. Add the scraps to a large pot with around 9 cups of water.**
2. **Get this going to a good simmer over medium heat. Add 1 teaspoon of salt and some pepper to give it a little more flavor. Add 2 bay leaves if you've got them. Let this all simmer together uncovered for around 1 hour to get all those flavors out.**
3. **Turn off the heat and then let the pot cool down. Strain out all the veggie scraps using a mesh strainer or some cheesecloth and you are good to go. You can freeze this broth for later, or store it in the fridge for up to a week. Throw your gallon bag back in the freezer and wait for it to fill up again.**

MISO PASTE

Miso paste is made of fermented soybeans and grains and comes in a fuckton of flavors. Because it's fermented, it's full of probiotics and all that good shit that helps your gut do its thing. Always add miso last to soup so you don't overheat it and kill all that good stuff. You can find it in the fridge at a well-stocked store or at your neighborhood Asian grocer. Yeah, take your ass down the street and try new things by supporting a local business, motherfucker.

VEGETABLE-NOODLE SOUP WITH GINGER MISO BROTH

Stop fucking with that deep-fried ramen and its foil-wrapped flavor fibs. This soup is perfect for when you feel a cold coming on but your ass is too worn out to cook. Take the few extra minutes to make this and put that ramen back in your zombie apocalypse kit where it fucking belongs.

MAKES 2 BIG-ASS BOWLS OR 4 SIDES

BROTH

4 inches fresh ginger
2 big cloves garlic
1 carrot
6 cups vegetable broth or water
10 sprigs cilantro*

NOODLES AND VEGGIES

8 ounces soba, udon, or rice noodles
¼ teaspoon soy sauce or tamari
1¼ cups broccoli cut into bite-size pieces
1½ teaspoons red miso paste**
1 carrot, cut into thin matchsticks
1 cup snow peas cut into matchsticks
⅓ cup thinly sliced green onions

Your favorite condiments***

1 To make the broth, peel the ginger by scraping the skin off with a spoon. Cut the ginger into ¼-inch-thick slices. Thickly slice the garlic too and chop the carrot into big chunks. Grab a medium pot and turn the heat on to medium. Once the pot is hot, add the ginger and carrot chunks and let those fuckers go on the bottom of the pot with no oil or anything. Keep stirring them around off and on for 2 minutes. It's cool if they stick, just rip them off with the spoon and keep going. Now add the garlic and do the same shit for another minute. Pour in the broth or water, add the cilantro, and let that veggie hot tub simmer for 15 minutes.

2 While the broth is doing its thing, cook the noodles according to the package directions.

3 When the broth has simmered 15 minutes, pull out all the ginger, garlic, carrot, and cilantro with a slotted spoon. Add the soy sauce and broccoli and simmer for a minute or two until the broccoli has lost its raw edge, then turn off the heat. Scoop up ½ cup of the broth and dissolve the miso paste in it, stirring until the chunks are gone. Pour that back in the pot and give it all a taste. Fucking great, right?

4 To assemble, grab a handful of the noodles and place them at the bottom of a bowl. Add a handful of the carrots, snow peas, and green onions. Ladle the hot broth and broccoli bits over and let it sit for a minute as the carrots and snow peas soften. Top with some more of the green onions and some of your favorite condiments.

* *Stems and all, bitches.*

** *WTF? See opposite page.*

*** *A squeeze of lime juice, a dash of toasted sesame oil, and a splooge of Sriracha are usually the way to go for condiments, but you do you.*

POZOLE ROJO

Part soup, part chili, pozole is a hearty dish that you can trick out with a fuckton of toppings.

MAKES ENOUGH FOR 6 HUNGRY PEOPLE, NO FUCKING PROBLEM

5 large dried chiles*
2 cups warm water
1 large onion
5 cloves garlic
1 zucchini
2 tablespoons unsweetened cocoa powder**
1 teaspoon olive oil
8 ounces tempeh
2 teaspoons soy sauce or tamari
1 can (29 ounces) hominy***
1 tablespoon dried oregano
2 teaspoons ground cumin
¼ teaspoon salt
5 cups vegetable broth
1 teaspoon maple syrup or other liquid sweetener
Juice of 1 lime
Toppings: Sliced cabbage, sliced green onions, radishes cut into matchsticks, cilantro, sliced avocado, lime wedges

1 Grab a big pot or griddle and toast the dried chiles on both sides until they get a little bendy and soft, about 2 minutes. Don't let these fuckers burn. Stay focused. When they are all good, throw them in a bowl with the warm water and let them soak for 15 to 20 minutes.

2 While that's going down, chop up the onion, garlic, and zucchini. When the chiles are nice and rehydrated take them out of the water but hold on to the water. Cut off the chile tops, remove the seeds, and chop them all up. Throw them in a blender or food processor with the water they were soaked in, the garlic, and cocoa powder, and run it until the chile-garlic paste looks all mashed up with no big chunks left.

3 Heat up the oil in a large soup pot over medium heat. Add the onion and sauté that shit for 2 minutes. Grab the tempeh and crumble that fucker right into the pot in dime- and nickel-size chunks and sauté until both the onion and tempeh start to brown, about 3 more minutes. Add soy sauce for a little flavor. Next, add the zucchini, hominy, oregano, cumin, and salt. Stir that all together and then add the chile-garlic paste you made earlier. Toss that all around so that everything is well coated and then add the broth. Cover that bastard and let it simmer for 15 to 20 minutes to get all the flavors to combine. Next add the maple syrup and lime juice. Taste that fucker and adjust the spices to the way you want it.

4 Serve hot with your favorite toppings.

* *Guajillo, ancho, whateverthefuck kind of big chiles you can find hanging at the end of the spice aisle.*

** *Yeah, the same shit you use to make brownies.*

*** *Hominy is made by soaking maize kernels in a lime mixture to soften their hulls, causing them to swell up. It is fucking awesome. You can buy hominy already cooked in cans near the beans and salsa at the store, or you can find it dried and cook it yourself like the package says.*

CAN'T DECIDE BETWEEN
CHILI OR SOUP?
FUCK IT
HAVE BOTH

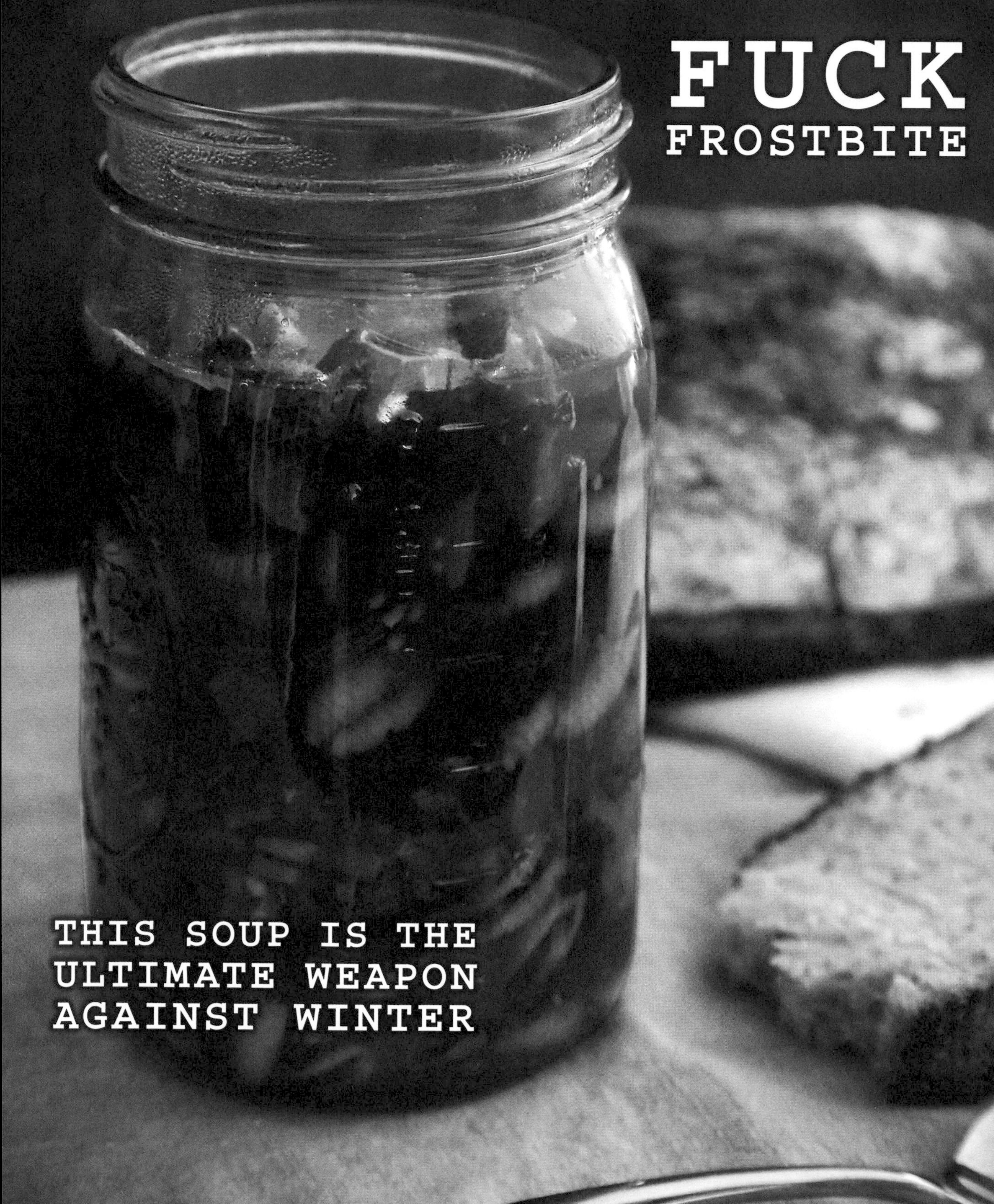
FUCK
FROSTBITE
THIS SOUP IS THE
ULTIMATE WEAPON
AGAINST WINTER

WARM THE FUCK UP MINESTRONE

This is a clean-out-the-fridge-style soup that will warm your ass up and keep you full for hours. Grab a mug, a thermos, or a big-ass bowl and get down. Enjoy with crusty bread if you like to eat in style.

MAKES ENOUGH FOR 4 TO 6

2 teaspoons olive oil
1 onion, chopped
2 carrots, sliced into half-moons
3 ribs celery, chopped
1 large potato or turnip, cut into dice-size pieces
2 teaspoons minced fresh rosemary
3 cloves garlic, minced
Pinch of red pepper flakes
1 bay leaf
1 can (14.5 ounces) low-salt diced tomatoes*
½ cup dried black lentils
7 cups vegetable broth
¼ teaspoon salt
1 cup small pasta shapes, like shells or stars or whatever
5 cups shredded green cabbage or kale
2 teaspoons red wine vinegar
Juice of ½ lemon
⅓ cup chopped fresh parsley
¼ cup minced fresh basil
Ground pepper

1 Grab a large soup pot and heat the oil over medium heat. Add the onion, carrots, and celery and sauté until the onion starts to look golden brown, 3 to 5 minutes. Add the potato, rosemary, garlic, pepper flakes, and bay leaf. Cook for another 30 seconds to get the garlic going. Add the diced tomatoes and lentils and give it another 30 seconds.

2 Now, pour in all the broth and let that motherfucker come to a simmer. Reduce the heat and let that go at a gentle pace until the lentils are almost cooked but the potato is tender, about 15 minutes. Next, add the salt, pasta, and cabbage (if using kale, don't add it yet) and keep the pot gently simmering until the pasta is cooked all the way, 5 to 10 minutes, depending on your pasta. (If you *are* using kale, fold it into the pot after the pasta is all cooked and let that pot simmer for 2 more minutes.)

3 Add the vinegar and lemon juice, stir well, and remove from the heat. Fold in the parsley and basil and let the pot sit for a minute or two. Taste to see whateverthefuck else it might need, like pepper or more rosemary to taste. Pull out the bay leaf and serve right away.

* *If tomatoes are in season and for some fucking reason you are making this soup, then sub in 3 fist-size tomatoes, chopped.*

SUMMER SQUASH SOUP

Don't skin the squash before you throw it in, because that's where most of its badass antioxidants hang out. That shit is just ignorant and wasteful.

MAKE ENOUGH FOR 4 AS A SIDE

- 1½ tablespoons olive oil
- ½ onion, chopped
- 2 ribs celery, chopped
- 1 carrot, sliced into thin half-moons
- 1 fist-size russet (baking) potato, chopped into dice-size cubes
- 3 large yellow squash, sliced into half-moons ⅛ inch thick
- 3 cloves garlic, minced
- ½ teaspoon salt
- 4 cups vegetable broth
- ⅓ cup sliced chives or green onions

1 In a large soup pot, heat the oil over medium heat. Add the onion, celery, and carrot and sauté until they begin to look a little golden, 3 to 5 minutes. Add the potato, squash, and garlic and cook for another 3 minutes. Add the salt and veggie broth and bring it to a simmer. Cook until the potato is tender, 10 to 15 minutes.

2 Turn off the heat. Use an immersion blender and blend until that son of a bitch looks nice and creamy and without a ton of chunks. (You could also pour it into a regular blender and do it that way. Just return the blended soup to the pot.) Bring it back up to a simmer. Turn off the heat, add the chives, and then taste. Add more salt, garlic, chives, your favorite shit. Serve right away.

CORN AND BASIL CHOWDER

Make this soup at the height of summer when corn is sweet and cheap as hell. Adding some basil at the last minute really makes this motherfucker taste like summer in a bowl.

MAKES ENOUGH FOR 4 TO 6 AS A SIDE

- 6 large ears corn, shucked
- ½ yellow onion
- 2 ribs celery
- 1 red bell pepper
- 1 medium russet (baking) potato
- 3 cloves garlic
- 2 teaspoons olive oil
- ½ teaspoon salt
- 4 cups vegetable broth
- 2 tablespoons lemon juice
- ¼ cup fresh basil leaves, sliced into ribbons

1 First you want to use a sharp knife to cut the corn off of the cobs. It's easier if you snap the cob in half, stand it on its end in the middle of a large bowl and cut the kernels off from top to bottom. When you're all done, you should have about 4 cups of kernels. Don't get lazy and use frozen corn here; that shit will not taste the same. Chop the onion, celery, bell pepper, and potato into bean-size pieces and mince the garlic. Prep work done.

2 Now grab a large soup pot and heat the oil over medium heat. Add the onion and cook until it browns lightly, about 3 minutes. Add the celery, bell pepper, potato, and garlic and cook for about 2 more minutes. Add the salt and then three-quarters of the corn kernels and stir. Add the broth and let that son of a bitch simmer until the potato pieces are soft, about 10 minutes.

3 When the potato is soft, turn off the heat. Use an immersion blender and blend until that motherfucker looks nice and creamy and without a bunch of chunks. (You could also pour it into your blender and do it that way; up to you. Just return the blended soup to the pot.) Add the rest of the corn and the lemon juice, and bring it back to a simmer. Turn off the heat, add the basil, and then taste. Add more salt, more lemon juice, more basil, whatever. Serve right away with some more basil on top to make that shit look as legit as it tastes.

POTATO LEEK SOUP

This soup is so damn tasty you won't believe the flavor came from so few things. It's kitchen witchcraft: kitchcraft.

MAKES ENOUGH FOR 4 AS A SIDE

- 3 fist-size russet (baking) or yellow potatoes*
- 3 medium leeks**
- 1 tablespoon olive oil
- 3 to 4 cloves garlic, minced
- 4 cups vegetable broth
- ¼ teaspoon salt
- ¼ teaspoon ground pepper
- ¼ cup sliced fresh chives or green onions
- ¼ cup chopped fresh dill

1 Chop the potatoes into 1-inch cubes. Keep the skin on if you like to go hard. Cut off the rough, leafy ends of the leeks and save that shit to make broth later (see page 86). Cut off the roots and then slice that fucker up the middle lengthwise. Now cut the leek crosswise into ribbons about as thin as a hair tie and wash the fuck out of them.

2 Heat the oil up in a stockpot over medium heat. Add the clean leeks and sauté those guys around until they start to soften up, 3 to 4 minutes. Add the potatoes and garlic and stir to combine. Pour in the vegetable broth and salt. Bring all of that to a boil, then cover it and reduce the heat to a simmer. Let that go until the potatoes are tender, about 15 minutes.

3 When everything is good and soft, you're going to want to blend the fuck out of it. You can let it cool for a bit and then add it to your blender, or you can stick your immersion blender right in there and get that shit down in a sec. Do whatever you can. Once the soup is nice and creamy, add it back to the pot (if you took it out), add the pepper, and warm it back up. Stir in the chives and taste. Add more salt and pepper if you think it needs it. That shit is on you. Dish that soup up and serve with about a tablespoon of the fresh dill on top. Tasty and classy.

* *About 1 pound*

** *Leeks are always dirty as hell when you buy them because they grow in sandy soil and can be hard to clean when they are whole. Instead, cut them up to the size you need them, throw them in a bowl of water, and mix that shit around so that all the dirt comes loose and sinks to the bottom. Drain it and rinse a couple more times so you aren't eating any grit with dinner.*

PUMPKIN CHILI

This isn't a weak-ass canned chili that needs fucking validation from some football players telling you how good it is. Hell no, this is hearty spoon-stands-up-on-its-own kind of shit.

MAKES ENOUGH FOR 4 TO 6 PEOPLE DEPENDING ON HOW MUCH THEY LIKE CHILI

1 yellow onion
1 carrot
1 bell pepper
1 teaspoon olive oil
2 to 3 cloves garlic, minced
1 jalapeño, minced
2 teaspoons soy sauce or tamari
2½ tablespoons mild chili powder
1 teaspoon dried oregano
1 teaspoon ground cumin
1 can (14.5 ounces) low-salt diced tomatoes*
1½ cups pureed pumpkin**
2 cups vegetable broth or water
3 cups cooked beans***
1 tablespoon lime juice
Toppings: cilantro, chopped onion, jalapeños, avocado, tortilla strips

1 Chop up the onion, carrot, and bell pepper into pieces no bigger than a bean.

2 In a big soup pot, heat the oil over medium heat. Add the onion, carrot, and bell pepper and sauté them until they begin to brown, about 5 minutes. Add the garlic, jalapeno, soy sauce, and spices and cook that all together for another 30 seconds. Add the tomatoes, pumpkin, broth, and beans and stir that up so everything is mixed. Get those flavors mingling and shit. Turn down the heat, cover, and let that simmer together for about 15 minutes. Stir it around every now and then.

3 When it is done simmering, turn off the heat and stir in the lime juice. Serve right away with your favorite toppings.

* *Fire-roasted tomatoes are damn delicious if you can find them.*

** *You can buy canned pumpkin puree or cut up a fresh pumpkin into chunks, steam it until it is tender, and puree the fuck out of it until you have 1½ cups. If you try to make this chili with pumpkin pie filling, don't complain about how fucked up it tastes. You did that dumb shit yourself.*

*** *Whatever beans you prefer in chili are cool, but if you need direction, half black bean and half pinto make a solid combo. And yeah, you can use two 15-ounce cans.*

TORTILLA SOUP

This old-school Southwestern soup is so goddamn good, even your grandma would approve. Just don't let her catch you swearing in the house.

MAKES ENOUGH FOR 4 AS A MAIN, 6 AS A SIDE

- 1 yellow or white onion
- 1 carrot
- 1 bell pepper
- 1 to 2 jalapeños
- 4 cloves garlic
- 1 tablespoon olive oil
- 2½ teaspoons each ground cumin, dried oregano, and chili powder
- ⅛ teaspoon salt
- 1 can (14.5 ounces) low-salt diced tomatoes*
- ¼ cup tomato paste
- 5 cups vegetable broth
- 1 tablespoon lime juice
- 6 to 8 corn tortillas, cut into 1-inch squares**
- 1½ cups cooked chickpeas***
- Toppings: Chopped cilantro, minced jalapeños, avocado, shake from the bottom of your tortilla chip bag

1 Chop up the onion, carrot, and bell pepper into pieces about the size of a chickpea. Mince the garlic and jalapeños. Now you're ready to get down to business.

2 Grab a large soup pot and sauté the onion in the oil until it starts to look a little see-through, about 2 minutes. Add the carrot and bell pepper and cook until everything is golden, another 3 minutes. Add the jalapeños, garlic, spices, and salt and cook for another 30 seconds. This should smell pretty goddamn dope right about now. Add the diced tomatoes and tomato paste. Make sure that you stir that son of a bitch around enough so that the paste isn't just sitting in a clump. Add the broth and let that all come to a simmer.

3 Now it's time to take this motherfucker up a notch. Add the lime juice and tortilla squares. Stir everything up and let that all gently simmer together until the tortillas get nice and soft, about 10 minutes. Now turn off the heat and grab your immersion blender and pulverize that bastard until it's nice and smooth. If you don't have an immersion blender, you can throw this all in your regular blender in batches too. Your call. Taste and add more of whatever you think it needs.

4 Serve this up with chickpeas piled in the center of each bowl, with chunks of avocado, some minced jalapeño, and some cilantro. Chip shake is welcome, too.

* *Regular or fire-roasted would be dope here.*

** *If you like a thicker soup, go with 8.*

*** *Or one 15-ounce can*

TRY NOT TO LICK THE FUCKING PAGE

IT TASTES NOTHING LIKE THE RECIPE

PREPARE FOR A
FUCKING
FOOD COMA

CHICKPEAS AND DUMPLINGS

This stew is thick and our personal favorite. If you've never had some version of this Southern staple, then GET THE FUCK ON IT. These dumplings are rolled out like delicious fluffy noodle things and not just those shitty drop dumplings other people use. Yeah, that's right. Shots fired in the dumpling wars.

MAKES ENOUGH FOR 6 HUNGRY MOTHERFUCKERS

DUMPLINGS

- **1 bunch of chives**
- **2 cups all-purpose flour***
- **2 teaspoons baking powder**
- **¾ teaspoon garlic powder**
- **¼ teaspoon salt**
- **½ to 1 tablespoon olive oil**
- **½ to 1 cup unsweetened plain almond milk**

* *Whole wheat flour is a little too dense for these fuckers, but give it a go if that's what you got and you are feeling brave.*

1 First thing, make the fucking dumplings. Chop up the chives into little pieces and set them aside. Add the flour to a medium bowl and whisk in the baking powder, garlic powder, and salt. Drizzle in the olive oil and mix it all up. Add ½ cup of the milk and stir it all together. If your dough still looks really dry, add a couple tablespoons of the rest of the milk until you can form a kind of shaggy ball. If you add too much milk, the dough will be sticky and hard to handle, so slow your ass down. Knead in ¼ cup of the chopped chives, making sure they are all mixed in and the dough looks like it has its shit together. (Set the rest of the chives aside.)

2 On a well floured surface, roll out the dough about ⅛ inch thick. (Think thin crust pizza.) Cut the dumplings into pieces about 1 inch wide and 1½ inches long. You will have some fucked up sizes because that's how shit is, but don't stress. They will be fine. You should get around 70 dumplings. Stack them up on a floured plate and stick them in the fridge uncovered. (Confused? See the photo on the next page.)

3 Make the soup: Remove the hard stems from the kale and slice those leaves into 1-inch ribbons. Set aside until the very end. In a large soup pot, heat up the 2 teaspoons oil over medium heat. Add the onions and a pinch of salt and sauté until the onions start to brown, 5 to 7 minutes. Add the carrots and celery and cook for another 3 minutes. Add the broccoli and garlic and cook until the carrots are getting soft but the broccoli still has some bite, another 3 minutes. Turn off the heat and dump all that shit into a medium bowl and set it aside. Make sure to scrape out all the veggies because you are reusing that pot. Fuck extra dishes.

(not even close to done; turn the damn page)

SOUP

5 to 7 leaves of kale**

2 sweet onions, chopped into bite-size pieces

2 carrots, chopped into bite-size pieces

3 ribs of celery, chopped into bite-size pieces

1 small crown of broccoli, chopped into bite-size pieces

3 to 4 cloves garlic, minced

2 teaspoons plus ¼ cup olive oil

Salt

2½ teaspoons dried oregano

1 teaspoon garlic powder

½ teaspoon ground black pepper

¼ teaspoon cayenne pepper

7 tablespoons all-purpose flour

½ cup white wine***

10 cups vegetable broth

3 cups cooked chickpeas****

1½ cups frozen green peas

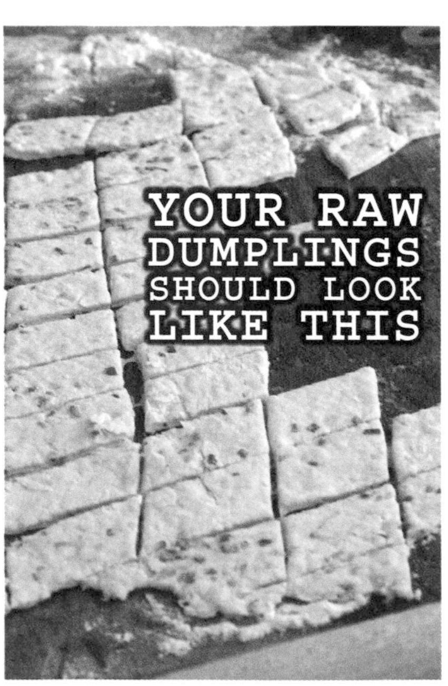
YOUR RAW
DUMPLINGS
SHOULD LOOK
LIKE THIS

4 Mix the oregano, garlic powder, black pepper, cayenne pepper, and ¼ teaspoon salt together in a small cup. Warm that soup pot back up over medium heat, add the remaining ¼ cup oil, and whisk in the flour. It should look somewhere between glue and runny paste. Yum? Keep stirring that shit around until it smells kinda nutty and looks a little toasted, about 2 minutes. Toss in the spice mixture and keep stirring for another 30 seconds. Whisk in the white wine. The flour will ball up with the wine and make it look like frosting or some shit like that. Slowly whisk in 2 cups of the broth. Mix that up until it is all incorporated and starts to look thick, like movie theater nacho cheese. Slowly whisk in the next 4 cups of broth and make sure it's smooth with no chunks of flour. Whisk in the remaining 4 cups broth and let it simmer, whisking every minute or so, for about 15 minutes. The broth should thicken up and start to look and taste kind of velvety. You know what the fuck we are talking about. Try it. Fucking awesomeness without 2 sticks of butter.

5 With the pot still simmering, add the dumplings a couple at a time so they don't get all stuck together in a clusterfuck of dough and dying dreams. Once they are all in, gently stir them around once so that everybody is bobbing around in the broth. Let them simmer together for 3 minutes so that the pot gets a chance to warm back up. Add the chickpeas and sautéed veggies and let them all simmer together for about 10 more minutes or until the dumplings don't taste raw.

6 Once your dumplings are on point, add the green peas and sliced kale. Yeah, that's right, just dump the peas in frozen because who gives a fuck? Cook for another 2 minutes so that the peas warm up and the kale wilts. Turn off the heat and throw in ¼ cup of those chives from earlier. Taste that shit and see if you want more herbs, spices, or salt to get it where you love it. Serve immediately and top the bowls with some of whatever chives you have left.

** *Spinach or collards will work here too.*

*** *Whateverthefuck you like to drink will work. Out of wine? Just use broth.*

**** *About two 15-ounce cans if you aren't cooking your own.*

WEDDING SOUP WITH WHITE BEAN BALLS AND KALE

Combining this soup's ingredients makes a flavor commitment so strong that it's in the fucking name. Once you taste it, you'll vow to never go another cold day without a bowl of this in your life.

MAKES ENOUGH FOR 6 PEOPLE WHO CAME HUNGRY

1 Crank your oven to 400°F. Coat a baking sheet with cooking spray.

2 Now, make the bean balls. Chop up the onion and measure out ¼ cup. Save the rest but push it to the side; we'll use that shit in a bit. Mash up the beans in a large bowl until they form a paste. Some whole bean bits are cool, but try to keep that shit to a minimum. Stir in the rest of the ingredients including the ¼ cup chopped onion and mix it all up so that everything gets distributed. You might need to use your hands to really get in there. Don't act like you're too cool to touch bean paste. If it feels a little dry, add a tablespoon or two of water. Roll the dough into balls about the size of a golf ball and put them on the greased up baking sheet. You should get 20 to 25 depending on your rollin' skills. Spray them with a little cooking spray and bake them for about 30 minutes, turning them over halfway, until both sides are golden brown.

3 While the balls are cooking, get your soup ready. In a large soup pot, heat the oil over medium heat. Add the rest of that onion from earlier (told ya), the carrots, and celery and sauté until the onion starts to brown, 3 to 5 minutes. Add the garlic and pasta and cook for 30 more seconds. Gently pour in the broth and let it all simmer together until the pasta is tender, 10 to 15 minutes. Fold in the lemon juice, greens, salt, pepper, and parsley and turn off the heat.

* *Or two 15-ounce cans. Kidney beans would work, too, but those motherfuckers are red and we didn't want to change the name of the recipe. Truth.*

** *WTF? See page 10.*

(turn the fucking page to keep reading)

WHITE BEAN BALLS

Cooking spray

1 large yellow onion

3 cups cooked white or cannellini beans*

½ cup whole wheat bread crumbs

3 cloves garlic, minced

¼ cup nutritional yeast or flour**

2 tablespoons olive oil

1 tablespoon soy sauce or tamari

2 teaspoons no-salt, all-purpose seasoning blend

1 teaspoon each dried thyme, basil, and oregano

½ teaspoon grated lemon zest

SOUP

1 teaspoon olive oil

2 carrots, chopped

2 ribs celery, chopped

3 cloves garlic, minced

1 cup small dried pasta**

9 cups vegetable broth

1 tablespoon fresh lemon juice

4 cups chopped kale or other dark, leafy greens

¼ teaspoon each salt and ground pepper

¼ cup chopped fresh parsley or basil

4 When everything is ready, place 3 or 4 bean balls in the bottom of a bowl and gently ladle the soup over them. Serve it up right away. The balls will slowly break apart as you eat and everything will taste so damn good together you'll understand why the fuck it's called wedding soup.

** *Orzo, elbows, stars, letters, whateverthefuck you got.*

QUALITY
CONTROL

PINATAS
DULCE
GLOBOS
JUGUETES
CENTRO DE MESAS
BAUTIZOS, BABY SHOWERS, BIRTHDAYS
TODO PARA SUS FIESTAS
TAP

the munchies

SALSAS, SIPS, AND THE SNACK LIFE

CUMIN-SPIKED PINTO BEAN DIP

Refried? Naw, we're not feeling that. How about ripped the fuck apart? Try this creamy bean dip and show those beans who's boss.

MAKES ENOUGH FOR 4 TO 6, ABOUT 3½ CUPS

2 teaspoons olive oil
1 white or yellow onion, chopped (about 1 cup)
1½ tablespoons ground cumin
¼ teaspoon cayenne pepper
3 cups cooked pinto beans*
½ cup vegetable broth or water
2 tablespoons lime juice
Salt

1 Heat the oil up in a sauté pan and cook the onions until they begin to brown around the edges, about 4 minutes. Add 1 tablespoon of the cumin and all of the cayenne pepper and cook for another 30 seconds. This part should smell pretty fucking good. Turn off the heat and let that mix cool for a minute.

2 Drop the onions, beans, broth, lime juice, and the last ½ tablespoon of the cumin into a food processor and let that fucker rip until it's creamy. No food processor? Just smash all that up until it has a consistency you can deal with. Taste and add a pinch or two of salt if you think it needs it.

* *Two 15-ounce cans if you're lazy*

WHITE BEAN AND ROSEMARY HUMMUS

If you're looking to up your protein intake, this makes a great sandwich spread and it's a hell of a lot better than some mayo misstep.

MAKES ENOUGH FOR 4 TO 6, ABOUT 4 CUPS

3 cups cooked white or cannellini beans*

¼ cup tahini**

¼ cup vegetable broth or water

3 tablespoons balsamic vinegar

2 cloves garlic, minced

1 tablespoon minced fresh rosemary

1 Add everything to a food processor or blender and let that shit run until it's nice and creamy. You know, aim for hummus-like. You could do this by hand with a potato masher but it will fucking take a while even if you are ripped.

2 Let it sit for 30 minutes in the fridge before serving so all those flavors can get acquainted.

* *Or two 15-ounce cans*

** *WTF is tahini?* *See page 32.*

*this is a puppy paw
Nintendo
1
2
3
4

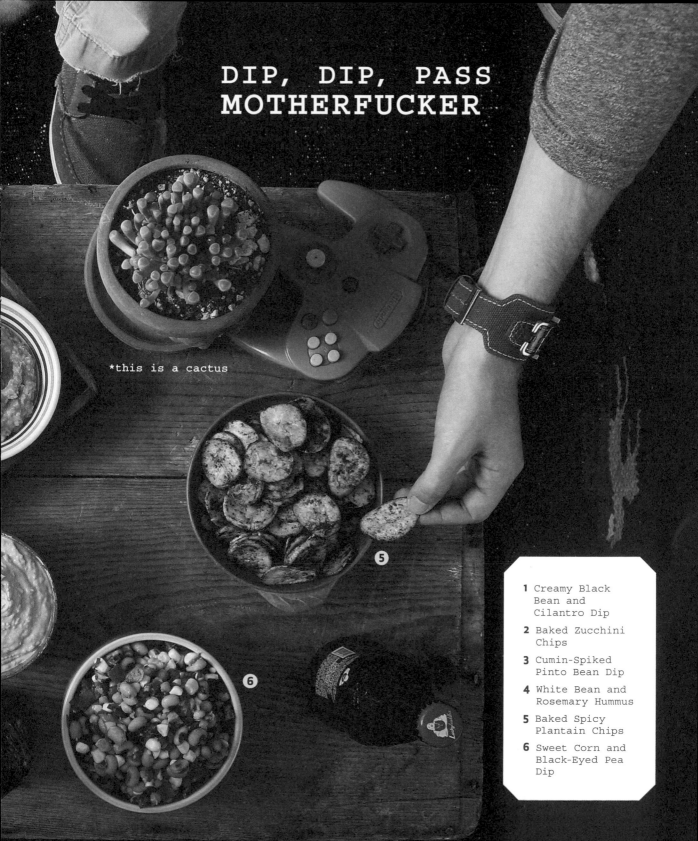

DIP, DIP, PASS MOTHERFUCKER

*this is a cactus

1 Creamy Black Bean and Cilantro Dip
2 Baked Zucchini Chips
3 Cumin-Spiked Pinto Bean Dip
4 White Bean and Rosemary Hummus
5 Baked Spicy Plantain Chips
6 Sweet Corn and Black-Eyed Pea Dip

SWEET CORN AND BLACK-EYED PEA DIP

Some people call this Texas Caviar. We just call it goddamn delicious. This makes a fuckton of dip, so if you're flying solo, just halve everything.

MAKES ENOUGH FOR 4 TO 6, ABOUT 5 CUPS

1 red bell pepper
1 small tomato
3 cups cooked black-eyed peas*
1 cup raw corn kernels**
½ cup sliced green onions
⅓ cup chopped cilantro
2 cloves garlic, minced
1 jalapeño, minced
2 tablespoons olive oil
2 tablespoons lime juice
2 tablespoons red wine vinegar
¼ teaspoon ground cumin
¼ teaspoon salt

1 Chop up the bell pepper and tomato into pieces about the size of a bean.

2 Add the black-eyed peas to a large bowl and smash them just a little bit. You want roughly one-third of them smashed up; the rest can stay whole. This just adds an extra creaminess to the dip, but you can skip it if you are over the whole mashed bean thing.

3 Mix in the pepper and tomato and everything else, stir, and taste. Easy. Add more lime juice or salt if you think it needs it. Serve this as a dip or over some greens for a fucking bomb-ass salad.

* *Two 15-ounce cans if you really don't like saving money.*

** *That should be about 1 cob's worth. Sigh.*

CREAMY BLACK BEAN AND CILANTRO DIP

This savory dip can elevate even the lamest party. YES, IT'S THAT FUCKING GOOD. It has the power to make you cool.

MAKES ENOUGH FOR 4 TO 6, ABOUT 3 CUPS

2½ cups cooked black beans*
⅓ cup vegetable broth or water
2 cloves garlic
Juice of 1 lime
Pinch of salt
½ teaspoon chili powder
¼ cup chopped cilantro
½ cup chopped green onions

Throw all of that shit in a food processor and run until creamy. Or mash the everliving fuck out of it with a potato masher until it is the consistency you want. Serve warm, room temperature, or cold. This is a dope spread for a wrap or sandwich, too.

* *Or 1⅔ 15-ounce cans*

BAKED ZUCCHINI CHIPS

In the middle of summer, most stores are practically giving away zucchini. Take advantage of that shit and make these chips. Snack like a goddamn king.

MAKES ENOUGH FOR 4 TO 6, ABOUT 30 CHIPS, DEPENDING ON THE SIZE OF YOUR ZUCCHINI. SO YEAH, SIZE MATTERS.

Cooking spray
1 medium zucchini, about 4 inches long and 1½ inches wide
1 tablespoon flour*
¼ teaspoon smoked paprika
¼ teaspoon garlic powder
Pinch of salt

1 Heat your oven to 350°F. Lightly coat a baking sheet with cooking spray.

2 Cut the zucchini into coins a little thicker than a quarter. If you cut them too thin they will burn the fuck up in the oven. If your slices start releasing some liquid, dab them with a towel to dry them off. Mix together the flour, paprika, garlic powder, and salt in a medium bowl. Toss in the zucchini and mix them together until all the zucchini pieces are coated in flavor.

3 Lay the zucchini on the baking sheet and coat the slices lightly with cooking spray. Bake for 30 to 40 minutes, flipping them over every 10 minutes, until they are all golden and crisp. Keep your eye on them because they can go from perfectly crispy to burnt to shit in a hot second. They are best served the day they are made so that crunch stays intact.

* *Whole wheat, white, rice, whatever you got is fine.*

BAKED SPICY PLANTAIN CHIPS

This is a chip with some motherfucking backbone. It's tasty as hell and won't break even in the heartiest of dips.

MAKES ENOUGH FOR 4 TO 6, ABOUT 30 CHIPS, DEPENDING ON THE SIZE OF THE PLANTAIN

Cooking spray
1 green plantain*
1 tablespoon olive or grapeseed oil
2 tablespoons lime juice
2 teaspoons chili powder
¼ teaspoon cayenne pepper
¼ teaspoon salt

1 Crank your oven to 400°F. Grab a baking sheet and coat it lightly with cooking spray.

2 Peel the plantain and cut it crosswise into slices no thicker than ⅛ inch. Don't measure that shit, just think *thin*.

3 Grab two bowls and put the oil and lime juice in one. Add the plantain and mix all around until every last motherfucking piece gets covered. Fish out the plantains and place them in the second bowl. Add the spices and salt and fucking mix that up until all the plantains have some seasoning on them.

4 Lay them out in a single layer on the baking sheet and bake them for 20 minutes, flipping them halfway. They will be golden and crispy when they are ready to go. They are best eaten the day they are made for crisp retention. Yeah that's right, *crisp retention*, some highbrow shit right there.

* *Plantains are like big, starchy bananas. Look for them in any market that specializes in Latin American foods.*

STOVETOP HERB POPCORN

When the hell did we all fall under the spell of microwave popcorn? SNAP THE FUCK OUT OF IT. Make your own, because it's cheaper and better for you. Win-win. Afraid you'll burn it? You already burn this shit in the microwave, so you really have nothing to lose.

MAKES ENOUGH FOR 4 TO 6, ABOUT 8 CUPS

HERB TOPPING

2 teaspoons nutritional yeast*

1 teaspoon dried basil

1 teaspoon dried thyme or dill

1 teaspoon garlic powder

⅛ teaspoon salt

POPCORN

1½ tablespoons high-heat oil like grapeseed or refined coconut oil

½ cup dried corn kernels

1½ tablespoons olive oil

⅛ teaspoon salt (optional)

1 Make the herb topping. Mix together the nutritional yeast, dried herbs, garlic powder, and salt in a small bowl.

2 Make the popcorn: In a large stockpot, heat the high-heat oil over medium heat. Add a couple kernels of corn, put on the lid, and shake it around every now and then. Once one of them pops that means your pan is ready. This might take up to a minute and a half.

3 When the pan is hot, add the rest of the kernels and cover that fucker up with a lid. If you have a glass lid, use that shit so you can spy on the corn. Shake the pan around every couple of seconds to keep those bitches from burning. It's like stirring without releasing all the heat. If they don't start popping within the first 30 seconds, turn your heat up just a bit. Soon it should sound like fucking firecrackers are going off in your kitchen. Once you hear more than a couple seconds between pops, turn off the heat. See, that took no time at all.

4 Pour the popcorn into a big bowl. Pour the olive oil all over that and stir it around to try and get a bunch covered. Sprinkle in that herb blend and toss it around. Taste and add another ⅛ teaspoon salt if that is your thing. This keeps for a couple days in an airtight container if you have the self-control.

* *This adds a vaguely cheesy taste to the popcorn and gives you that B_{12} boost. Still like WTF? See page 10.*

POP OFF
LIKE YOU MEAN IT

SPICY PICKLED CARROTS

This is a salsa bar staple around these parts. Serve these alongside your favorite tacos or burritos and nobody will say shit except thanks.

MAKES ENOUGH FOR 4 TO 6, OR ONE LARGE JAR

1 Cut the carrots and jalapeños into coins no thicker than ¼ inch.

2 In a saucepan, bring the vinegars, herbs, spices, onion, garlic, and salt to a boil on the stovetop. Add the carrots and jalapeños and simmer until they are slightly tender but still have some crunch, 3 to 5 minutes. Turn off the heat and pour into a large glass jar with a tight-fitting lid. Any old spaghetti sauce jar would work.

3 Let it sit at least 8 hours or overnight before serving. Will keep for at least 3 weeks in the fridge.

½ pound carrots
2 jalapeños
¾ cup distilled white vinegar
½ cup apple cider vinegar
1 teaspoon dried oregano
1 bay leaf
½ teaspoon cumin seeds
¼ teaspoon ground pepper
¼ cup slivered white or red onion
2 cloves garlic, smashed
¼ teaspoon salt

UPGRADE YOUR FRIDGE
INSTANTLY
JUST BY HAVING
THIS SHIT
IN THERE AT ALL TIMES

QUICK PICKLED CUCUMBERS AND ONIONS

These quick pickles go great with a breakfast bowl (Brown Rice Bowl with Edamame and Tamari Scallion Sauce, page 11), the Spring Veggie Bowl (page 177), or tossed in a salad with Toasted Sesame Dressing (page 35).

MAKES ENOUGH FOR 4 TO 6, ABOUT 2 CUPS

1 medium cucumber
¼ medium red onion
½ teaspoon salt
½ cup rice vinegar
1 tablespoon apple cider vinegar

1 Cut your cucumber in half lengthwise. Skin on or off, your call. Then cut each half into a bunch of half-moons no thicker than ¼ inch. Cut the onion into wire-coat-hanger-thin strips no longer than 2 inches.

2 Throw the cucumber and onion slices into a medium bowl, sprinkle them with the salt, and rub that all in with your hands. You could use a spoon if you are too fucking cool for school, but why? Pour in the vinegars and toss.

3 Cover this up and stick it in the fridge for 30 minutes. Stir it around and let it sit for at least another 30 minutes before it's go time. They will keep in the fridge for about a week.

MID-SUMMER SALSA

An old-school pico de gallo-style salsa. When tomatoes are in season there is no better snack than this shit right here.

MAKES ENOUGH FOR 4 TO 6, ABOUT 4½ CUPS

If you're a picky motherfucker about salsa, you've got a couple options here. Mix everything together in a bowl and leave it chunky, or throw everything in a food processor and run that shit until you get the consistency your ass prefers. Maybe you like your salsa chunky, maybe not. If salsa is being served, who really gives a fuck about consistency? Chill at least 20 minutes before serving.

* *About 1 lime*

1 pound tomatoes, chopped (about 2 cups)

½ white onion, chopped (about ½ cup)

2 to 3 cloves garlic

1 jalapeño, diced

2 tablespoons lime juice*

1 tablespoon orange juice (optional)

¼ cup chopped cilantro

½ teaspoon salt

*fire-roasted salsa
*grilled peach salsa

GRILLED PEACH SALSA

This salsa lets people know you aren't fucking around with your snack spread. The perfect combo between savory and sweet, this is one salsa that makes it hard to not double-dip.

MAKES ENOUGH FOR 4 TO 6, ABOUT 3½ CUPS

6 peaches (about 3 pounds)
½ teaspoon oil*
1 to 2 serrano peppers, minced
½ medium red onion, chopped (about ⅔ cup)
1 medium tomato, chopped
Juice of 2 limes (about ¼ cup)
¼ teaspoon salt
Handful of cilantro

1 Cut the peaches into wedges no thicker than an inch. You can leave the skin on because everybody needs more fiber in their motherfucking diet. You should get around 12 wedges out of each peach. Throw the cut-up peaches in a large bowl with the oil and mix them all together.

2 Bring your grill to a medium-high heat. Place the peaches on there for 45 seconds or so on each side. You don't need to cook them; you just want some char marks on there because that looks pro as fuck. Grilling the peaches also caramelizes their natural sugars, making them sweeter.

3 When the all peaches are grilled, let them cool for a couple minutes while you chop everything else up. When the peaches have cooled enough to handle, chop them up into salsa-appropriate-size pieces and then mix everything together. Let this all chill together for at least 30 minutes and then serve.

* *Grapeseed, regular sesame oil, or even olive oil would work here.*

FIRE-ROASTED SALSA

This is the salsa you make when tomatoes aren't in season and canned is your best bet. Otherwise, make the Mid-Summer Salsa (page 121) with your ripe tomatoes and save this for winter.

MAKES ENOUGH FOR 4 TO 6, ABOUT 2½ CUPS

- 1 can (14.5 ounces) fire-roasted diced tomatoes
- ½ white onion, chopped (about 1 cup)
- ⅓ cup chopped green onions
- ½ cup chopped cilantro
- 3 serrano peppers, chopped*
- 8 cloves roasted garlic**
- ¼ teaspoon ground cumin
- Juice of ½ lime
- Salt to taste

Throw all that in a food processor or blender and blend it until it's how you like it. Chunky, smooth . . . your salsa = your rules. Taste and add more lime juice if you think it needs it. Serve chilled or at room temperature. Keeps for about 4 to 5 days in the fridge, but your willpower probably won't allow for any leftovers.

* *You can remove the seeds if you aren't down with a hot salsa.*

** *Yeah, that's basically a whole bulb. Roasted garlic is broken down in "How to Roast Garlic" (page 40), but you can use 2 or 3 cloves of raw garlic if you are having a salsa emergency.*

SWEET FRESH HERB SALSA

This shit right here is not your standard salsa. It walks that line between sweet and savory but is addictive as hell. Throw it on some lentil tacos (page 144), use it as a dip for veggies, or toss it with some cold noodles for a simple side. Get on it.

MAKES ABOUT ¾ CUP

- 1 cup torn basil leaves
- ½ cup chopped cilantro
- ½ cup sliced green onions
- 1 jalapeño, minced*
- 1 clove garlic, minced
- 3 tablespoons rice vinegar
- 1 tablespoon orange juice
- 1 tablespoon lime juice
- 1 tablespoon olive oil

Throw everything together in a food processor and let that bitch run until everything is minced up. No food processor? Just mince everything up extra tiny by hand and mix that shit in a cup. Done.

* *Take out the seeds if you can't stand the heat..*

DROPPING KNOWLEDGE

USE ACIDS, NOT SALT

If you're cooking at home and your dish tastes flat as fuck, don't reach for the salt. Right now you're probably consuming entirely too much of those white crystals and your body can't hang. The Institute of Medicine says Americans eat 3,400 milligrams of sodium every damn day, a lot of it hidden in processed food and shit, when you really should be at 1,500 to 2,300. FUUUUCCCK THAT.

Instead, try adding a little acid. Citrus juice and vinegar can fix your cooking in ways salt can't touch. Flavors taste brighter and dishes feel more like restaurant-level shit. Just squeeze a lemon or give that vinegar bottle a shake or two. Aim for a teaspoon at first, but taste as you go. If you accidently overdo it with the acid, just add a little oil or sugar to the dish and balance it right the fuck out. Here are a few suggestions for some flavor combos, but be creative and try shit on your own:

- **Tomato-based dishes:** balsamic vinegar, red wine vinegar, or lemon juice
- **A dish with lots of fresh herbs like cilantro, dill, or parsley:** lemon juice, lime juice, or red wine vinegar
- **Dishes flavored with soy sauce/toasted sesame oil:** rice vinegar or orange, lemon, or lime juice
- **Bean-based dishes:** apple cider vinegar, sherry vinegar, balsamic vinegar

If you've done your job as a cook, then you shouldn't need the fucking salt shaker at the dinner table. So keep that shit in the kitchen as an ingredient, not a fucking condiment.

SALSA VERDE

This green monster brings all the fucking flavor to our chilaquiles (page 4) and will do the same for whatever lucky food you pour it on.

MAKES ENOUGH FOR 4 TO 6, ABOUT 2½ CUPS

1½ pounds tomatillos*
2 jalapeños
½ white onion, chopped
2 cloves garlic, minced
¼ cup chopped cilantro
1 tablespoon lime juice
⅛ teaspoon salt

1 Turn on the broiler in your oven and get it nice and hot.

2 Tear off all that loose, papery skin on the tomatillos and wash away all that sticky shit left on the fruit. Put the tomatillos and jalapeños in a baking dish with sides and throw it under the broiler.

3 Roast until the tomatillos are starting to blacken on top and the peppers are slightly charred, 10 to 15 minutes. Flip those fuckers around halfway through roasting so that they get a little roasted on all sides.

4 Once the tomatillos and jalapeños are cool enough to touch, roughly chop them up. If you like a spicier salsa, leave the seeds in the jalapeños, otherwise fish those fuckers out as you chop.

5 In a food processor, combine the tomatillos, jalapeños, onion, garlic, cilantro, lime juice, and salt and run that shit until you get a nice slightly chunky constancy, about 30 seconds.

6 Serve the salsa warm, at room temperature, or cold.

* *They aren't the same shit as green tomatoes. They have a papery outside skin that you peel away. Look for them in the fridge at a market that specializes in Mexican and Central American foods.*

PINE-APPLE GUACAMOLE

Not like guacamole really needs help being more delicious, but if you ever feel like mixing shit up, try this. The pineapple is so fucking dope that you may not want to share.

MAKES ENOUGH FOR 4 TO 6, ABOUT 2½ CUPS

- 2 avocados
- ⅔ cup chopped pineapple*
- ½ cup chopped red onion
- 2 tablespoons chopped cilantro
- 2 to 3 cloves garlic, minced
- Grated zest of ½ lime
- 1 tablespoon lime juice
- ⅛ teaspoon ground cumin
- Pinch of salt

Mash up the avocado into nice chunks. Add everything to the avocado and stir. Taste and add more of your favorite shit. Serve at room temp or chill. Eat this the day you make it. Why the fuck would you wait?

* *Fresh or canned is cool.*

AIN'T NO HEARTBREAK
LIKE CHIP SHAKE

ROASTED SRIRACHA CAULIFLOWER BITES WITH PEANUT DIPPING SAUCE

Buffalo bites with bones are a waste of flavor space and snacking time. Make some spicy cauliflower bites for your next party and double your snacking efficiency.

MAKES ENOUGH FOR 4 TO 6 PEOPLE, OR 1 PERSON WITH NO FEARS ABOUT WHAT THE CONSEQUENCES OF CONSUMING THAT MUCH HOT SAUCE COULD MEAN FOR THEIR ASSHOLE

2 medium heads cauliflower (about 2 pounds)

½ cup flour*

½ cup water

HOT SAUCE

2 teaspoons oil**

½ to ⅔ cup Sriracha or similar-style hot sauce***

¼ cup rice vinegar

½ teaspoon soy sauce or tamari

PEANUT DIPPING SAUCE

¼ cup warm water

¼ cup plus 2 tablespoons creamy peanut butter

2 tablespoons rice vinegar

2 tablespoons lime juice

2 teaspoons minced fresh ginger

1 teaspoon soy sauce or tamari

1 teaspoon maple syrup or agave syrup

1 cucumber, cut into finger-long sticks

1 Crank your oven to 450°F. Lightly grease a rimmed baking sheet. Chop up your cauliflower into little trees no bigger than your thumb.

2 Whisk together the flour and water in a big bowl until a batter forms with no chunks. Did you already fuck up and it's all chunky? Start that shit over again. Toss in the cauliflower and mix it around until all the pieces look a little coated. Spread the cauliflower out on the baking sheet and roast for 15 minutes. Mix those fuckers around halfway through roasting so all the sides get a little love.

3 Make the hot sauce. In a small saucepan, mix the oil, Sriracha, vinegar, and soy sauce. Heat that over a low heat until the sauce is warm but not bubbling. Turn off the heat and leave it alone.

4 Now it's time for the peanut dipping sauce. In a medium glass, whisk together the water and peanut butter until it looks all creamy. Add all the other ingredients and keep stirring until everything is incorporated. Stick that in the fridge until it's go time.

5 After 15 minutes in the oven, dump the cauliflower back in a big bowl and toss it with the hot sauce mixture from the stovetop. Make sure everything is coated. Drop those motherfuckers back on the baking sheet, leaving the extra sauce in the bowl, and roast for another 3 minutes just so everything is warm and delicious.

6 Serve hot or at room temperature with the cucumber sticks and peanut dipping sauce on the side.

* *All-purpose, whole wheat, or brown rice flour all work here. Use what you got.*

** *Olive oil, coconut oil, or grapeseed oil are cool.*

*** *If you like it hot, go for the ⅔ cup.*

WITH A
SNACK
LIKE THIS
EVERYBODY
FUCKING
WINS

IF A PEACH PIE,
MINT JULEP, AND
SUN TEA HAD A
THREE-WAY
YOU'D GET THIS
REFRESHING
FUCKER

PEACH-MINT SUN TEA

If you make this refreshing motherfucker when peaches are at their peak, you won't need to sweeten it at all.

MAKES ENOUGH FOR 4 PEOPLE OR 1 THIRSTY MOTHERFUCKER

- 4 cups cold water
- 4 bags of your favorite black tea
- 2 ripe peaches, peeled (or not) and chopped into chunks
- 2 tablespoons lemon juice
- 10 mint leaves, plus mint sprigs for garnish
- 2 teaspoons agave or maple syrup (optional*)
- Ice

1 Place the water and tea bags in a large container with a lid and set that fucker in the sun for 3 to 5 hours. No sunny spots where you stay? Just throw it in the fridge or leave it on the counter; it will still work.

2 Once the tea has steeped, get to making your drinks. Throw the peaches in a blender with the lemon juice, mint, and agave (if using). Add the tea and run that shit until everything is mixed and there aren't any peach chunks flying around. Taste and add more sweetener if you need it.

3 Pour over ice and serve with a sprig of mint in each glass. If you have a porch, go out there and enjoy this shit while you judge the neighbors.

* *Only add this if your peaches aren't super ripe.*

WATERMELON HIBISCUS COOLERS

Sip on this ice-cold glass and tell the summer sun to knock off that triple digit bullshit.

MAKES 4 GLASSES

6 cups cubed watermelon*

1½ cups brewed hibiscus tea, cooled**

Juice of 1 lime

2 to 3 teaspoons agave syrup or your favorite liquid sweetener

1 Throw the watermelon on a rimmed baking sheet and put it in the freezer for at least 1 hour.

2 When the watermelon is nice and frozen, add it to a blender with the rest of the ingredients. Blend that all up until it is smooth. Taste and add more sweetener if you think it needs it.

* *Seedless is ideal, but a couple of big seeds aren't a deal breaker.*

** *You could sub ¼ cup of this with some tequila if you want to party.*

FUCK OFF, SUN

WE'RE BUSY

GINGER-LIME SPARKLERS

No need to sit on your ass waiting around for syrups to boil and cool. You can have this fizzy ginger limeade ready in less than 5 minutes. Take your thirst from parched to quenched in no time. The tiny umbrellas are optional.

MAKES ENOUGH FOR 4

1 lime, cut into small wedges
1½ tablespoons minced fresh peeled ginger
3 tablespoons sugar or agave syrup
2 cups water
3 cups tonic water

1 Grab your blender and throw the lime wedges, ginger, sugar, and 1 cup of the water right in. Yeah, the whole fucking lime, rind and everything. Just have some faith. Now run that shit on high for about 1 minute so the lime is chopped up as much as possible and that sugar gets to break down.

2 Place a fine-mesh sieve or some cheesecloth over a pitcher and strain everything from the blender right in. Throw away the strained pulp. Add the remaining 1 cup water and stir.

3 Now if you want to make a whole pitcher, just add the tonic water and kick back. But if you're making these motherfuckers by the glass, you'll want about ¾ cup tonic water for every ½ cup of lime mix. Done and done. And if you're thinking of adding a shot or 2 of gin or vodka, that shit would certainly help you relax.

CLINK BITCHES

*chocolate chip and almond butter cookies are a dope pairing. See page 195.

BLENDED EARL GREY LATTES

Maybe you want some tea, but it's just too goddamn hot outside for all that. Well, keep a jar of this shit in the back of your fridge for whenever you need a creamy caffeinated cool down. The tea mix will keep in the fridge for at least a week.

MAKES 2 TALL DRINKS

2 cups vanilla almond milk

½ cup water

4 bags Earl Grey tea*

1 to 2 teaspoons maple syrup or agave syrup (to taste)

2 cups ice cubes (about 12 cubes)

½ banana, cut into chunks and frozen**

1 In a small saucepan, heat the almond milk and water over medium heat until it starts to bubble around the edges. Turn off the heat and add the tea bags. Let them steep for 10 minutes while you do something incredibly unproductive. If you let the tea steep too long it could taste bitter, so set a fucking timer. Take the bags out and stick all that in the fridge to cool down for at least 1½ hours.

2 When you're ready to drink, add the maple syrup, ice, banana, and tea mix to a blender and run until it is smooth.

* *Honestly you can use chai, yerba maté, peppermint, whateverthefuck tea you like to drink. Go crazy.*

** *This sweetens it up and helps it get creamy. It's a good idea to keep a bag of peeled, frozen banana chunks in the freezer for moments like this.*

CREAMY HORCHATA

Almonds and rice team up to make this frosted drink creamy as fuck. Pour yourself a glass, put your feet up, and let your work wait while you chill out.

MAKES ABOUT 4 GLASSES

- 1 cup uncooked long-grain brown rice*
- $^2/_3$ cup raw almonds
- 3-inch cinnamon stick
- 4 cups water
- 1 tablespoon agave syrup or maple syrup**
- Ice or water
- Ground cinnamon

1 Rinse the rice well under cool water. Throw it in a large container with a lid and add the almonds, cinnamon stick, and water. Let this all soak together overnight or for at least 8 hours.

2 When that soaking is done, dump the whole deal in your blender, water and all, add the agave, and blend that mess until it's all smooth. Leave the cinnamon in—don't worry, that shit will blend up too. Pour it all through a fine-mesh strainer or cheesecloth to get out the grit.

3 If you are going to serve it right away, add 1 cup ice and blend it again to cool it down. If not, blend in another $^1/_2$ cup water and stick it in the fridge. Serve cold with ice cubes and some cinnamon sprinkled on top because you're fucking fancy like that.

* *Brown basmati rice is the best here, but use whatever the fuck kind of brown rice you can find.*

** *Whatever liquid, syrupy sweetener you got should do.*

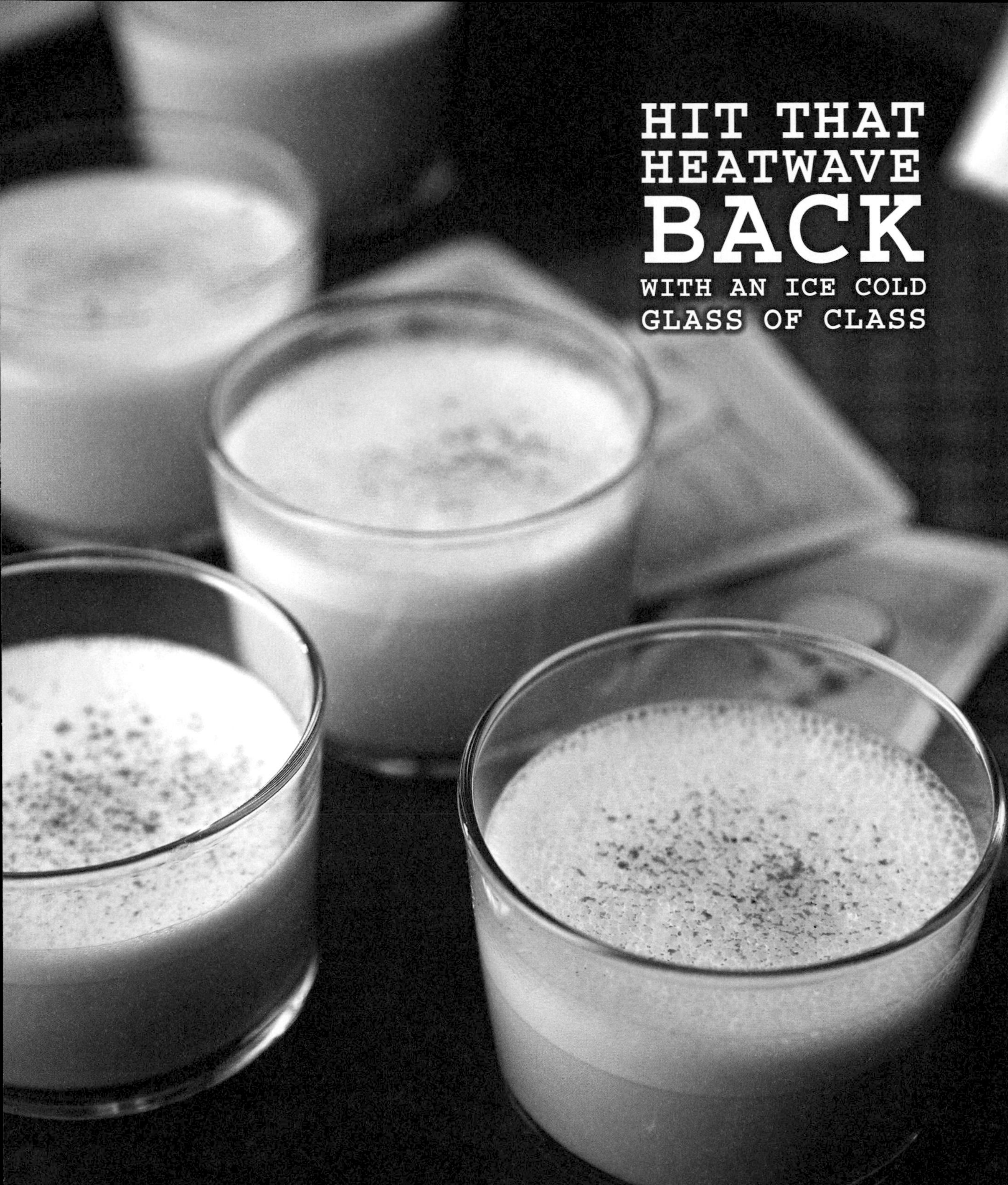
HIT THAT
HEATWAVE
BACK
WITH AN ICE COLD
GLASS OF CLASS

966

the main event

BURRITOS, BOWLS, AND OTHER
BOMB-ASS MEALS

BLACK BEAN TORTAS WITH COCONUT CHIPOTLE MAYO

Make this motherfucker STAT and see what your narrow sandwich world has been missing.

MAKES 4 TORTAS

1 First, make the mayo. Throw all those mayo ingredients in your blender or food processor and run that motherfucker on high for about a minute so everything is good and mixed. Taste and see if you want more hot sauce. Pour this all in a cup or bowl and store it in the fridge until you need it. It will thicken in there, just fucking be patient.

2 Next, make the beans. Heat the oil in a large soup pot over medium heat. Throw in the onion and sauté it until it starts to look golden brown, about 5 minutes. Add the garlic, chili powder, and cumin and cook for another 30 seconds. Add the beans and broth and stir that shit up. Let it come to a simmer and then turn down the heat real low. Using a potato masher or big-ass spoon, smash up all those beans as best you can. Think chunky guacamole. Add the lime juice and then taste. Add some salt or more spices if that's the kinda shit you're into. Now turn off the heat and make a torta.

3 Grab a toasted roll and smear with a bunch of the coconut chipotle mayo. Pile a fuckton of the beans on the bottom half. In between, add whateverthefuck you want. Lettuce, tomatoes, red onion, and some avocado are some time-tested choices, but be creative and shit. Serve right away with some extra hot sauce.

* *Yeah, chia seeds, like the fucking chia pet. They are rich in omega-3s and full of fiber. If you can't find them, flaxseeds are an OK sub.*

** *Two 15-ounce cans will do if you are in a rush.*

COCONUT CHIPOTLE MAYO

1 cup canned coconut milk

⅓ cup of your favorite chipotle hot sauce

¼ cup olive oil

1 tablespoon ground chia seeds*

1 teaspoon lemon juice

½ teaspoon garlic powder

Pinch of salt

CREAMY BLACK BEANS

1 teaspoon oil

1 yellow onion, chopped

3 cloves garlic, minced

1 tablespoon chili powder

¾ teaspoon ground cumin

3 cups cooked black beans**

1½ cups vegetable broth

Juice of 1 lime

Salt to taste

TORTA TRIMMINGS

4 crusty rolls, split and toasted

Lettuce

Sliced tomatoes

Sliced red onion

Sliced avocado

A TORTA IS A BADASS SANDWICH WITH THE SOUL OF A BURRITO

LENTIL TACOS WITH CARROT-JICAMA SLAW

A little sweet and a little savory, these bad bitches break all the taco rules. Serve them up with a side of the Creamy Peanut Slaw (page 71) and blow your taste buds back.

MAKES 6 TO 8 TACOS

LENTILS

3 cups water
1 cup black lentils,* rinsed
½ teaspoon olive oil
½ onion, chopped
8 ounces mushrooms, ** cut into bite-size pieces
1 tablespoon soy sauce or tamari
2 or 3 cloves garlic, minced
2 tablespoons apple juice***
1 teaspoon toasted sesame oil

CARROT-JICAMA SLAW

½ pound jicama****
1 small cucumber
1 carrot
2 tablespoons rice vinegar
1 tablespoon lime juice
¼ teaspoon salt

Sweet Fresh Herb Salsa (page 124)

1 For the lentils: Bring the water to boil in a medium saucepot over high heat and add the lentils. Turn the heat to low and simmer until tender, about 30 minutes. Drain the excess water and set aside.

2 In a large wok or skillet, heat the oil over medium heat and add the onion. Cook until the onion becomes translucent, about 3 minutes. Add the mushrooms and cook until they release some of their liquid, about 3 minutes. Add the soy sauce, stir, and then add the lentils. Mix that shit up and then add the garlic and apple juice. Yes, fucking apple juice. Just do it. Cook until most of the liquid has evaporated, about 2 minutes. Turn off the heat and stir in the toasted sesame oil. Taste that shit. Fucking awesome.

3 Now, the slaw. Cut the jicama, cucumber, and carrot into matchsticks no more than 1 inch long. Toss with the rest of the slaw ingredients and refrigerate before you serve it up.

4 To make the tacos, warm the tortillas and fill those gifts from god with the lentil mix, some shredded cabbage or lettuce, the jicama slaw, and top with that herb salsa. These fuckers aren't half bad cold either if you are feeling too lazy to heat up leftovers. Cold tacos are still motherfucking tacos.

* *These little bastards (also called beluga lentils—because they look like caviar) hold their shape better than other lentils, so look for them.*

** *Button, cremini, or shiitake mushrooms are cool. Use whatever.*

*** *The real shit, not apple-flavored drink.*

**** *This is a big-ass root that tastes so fucking good. It's like the product of a one-night stand between an apple and a potato. Don't fight it, just buy it.*

LENTILS
NEVER HAD IT
SO GOOD

DROPPING KNOWLEDGE

LUBE UP: HEALTHY OILS

As you fill up your pantry, you want to make sure you are grabbing all the best shit for you and your recipes. Oil is the first thing to hit the pan in so many meals so you best choose wisely. When it comes to cooking and baking, not all oils are created equal. Some oils are better for low-heat stuff like sautéing while some really shine when you are stir-frying and baking. You want to know the difference so that you choose the best shit for your dish. Oils that are better for high-heat cooking have a higher smoke point. So if you see your oil smoking, you are fucking shit up. When oils start to smoke, they start to break down and release free radicals and a bunch of other garbage that isn't so good for your health. Just heat your oils up until they shimmer and then get to cooking.

On top of function, you also want to know if your oil is adding any awesome flavors to your dish. We got you. Check the lists below and get your oil game under control.

Oils to Avoid

Right out the gate, don't go buying shit like this. Most of these oils are highly refined and offer no nutritional trade-off. Grab something else and get your money's worth.

- Vegetable oil
- Vegetable shortening (particularly if it is full of partially hydrogenated oils)
- Canola oil

Oils to Cook With over Low to Medium Heats

- Olive oil
- Unrefined coconut oil (this one tastes like coconuts, stable at room temp)
- Any of the high-heat oils (see below)

Oils to Cook With over High Heat

- Sesame oil
- Refined coconut oil (no coconut taste, stable at room temp)
- Grapeseed oil
- Peanut oil
- Safflower oil

Oils for Drizzling, Dressings, and Extra Flavor

- Extra virgin olive oil
- Walnut oil
- Toasted sesame oil

If you are looking for an oil that is solid at room temperature for things like pie crusts and biscuits, just grab some refined coconut oil and get to business. Stop looking around at other shit. Now go and cook up some delicious meals or quiz your fucking family on oils and look smart.

CREAMY RAVIOLI WITH HOUSE MARINARA

Making these fuckers for someone is an impressive feat and is sure to look extra sexy on a date. Nothing says "Let's take this to the bedroom" faster than stuffed pasta.

MAKES ABOUT THIRTY 2-INCH RAVIOLI

PASTA DOUGH*

2 cups all-purpose flour

½ cup whole wheat pastry flour

Pinch of salt

¾ to 1 cup water

3 tablespoons olive oil

House Marinara (page 148)

Tofu Ricotta (page 149)

1 To make the dough: In a large bowl, combine the flours and salt and stir it all around. Make a crater in the center of that and add ¾ cup of the water and the olive oil. Mix the liquids and flour together until a shaggy dough comes together. If there's still a bunch of dry-ass flour in the bowl, add the remaining ¼ cup water—but no more—1 tablespoon at a time until that shit comes together (it should be a little drier and less sticky than pizza dough). Once you've got your ball of dough, knead it on a well-floured surface for 10 minutes so that shit gets nice and elastic. If you don't do this, your dough will be pasty and gross, so don't get lazy. Place the dough back in the bowl, cover, and let it rest in the fridge for at least 30 minutes but up to 2 hours.

2 While the dough is resting, prepare the tofu ricotta and marinara.

3 To form the ravioli, you'll need a ravioli stamp.** First, cut the dough in half. On a well-floured surface, roll out one piece to a rough rectangle that's twice the width of your ravioli stamp and about ⅛ inch thick. With a short end of the rectangle facing you, use the stamp to imprint the dough with 2 side-by-side ravioli squares, fitting about 15 of these pairs down the length of the rectangle. Fill each ravioli imprint on the left-hand side with 1 tablespoon of the tofu ricotta. Using a pastry brush or paper towel, wet the dough along the edges of all the stamps and fold the right-hand row over the left so that all the stamps line up and the filling is completely covered (see page 149 for a pic). Stamp over each ravioli again until they are sealed, then transfer to a large baking sheet. Repeat this process with the other piece of dough. (At this point you can either freeze the ravioli or cook them immediately.)

(Hold the fuck up, we're not done yet—turn the page)

* *If you're feeling lazy as fuck or are scared of making your own dough, you can cheat and just buy wonton wrappers and use them instead. Skip the whole ravioli stamp and rolling out thing. Just place a little filling in the center of a wonton wrapper, wet the edges, and press another wrapper over the top, making sure to seal the edges. Freeze them or cook them right away just like the homemade shit.*

** *That ravioli stamp shouldn't be more than a couple bucks at the store and it'll make this whole fucking process easier. Or you can use a knife and just cut those bastards out if you are feeling brave. Just remember to wet your fingers and press down the edges so the filling doesn't spill out while you cook.*

4 To cook, bring a large pot of salted water to boil and add the ravioli in batches of 8 to 10, depending on the size of your pot. Boil gently until the raviolis float, 2 to 4 minutes.

5 Serve with the marinara.***

*** *Or just serve with your favorite sauce or with the basil pesto from the Mixed Mushroom and Spinach Lasagna (page 150) thinned out with a couple tablespoons of water.*

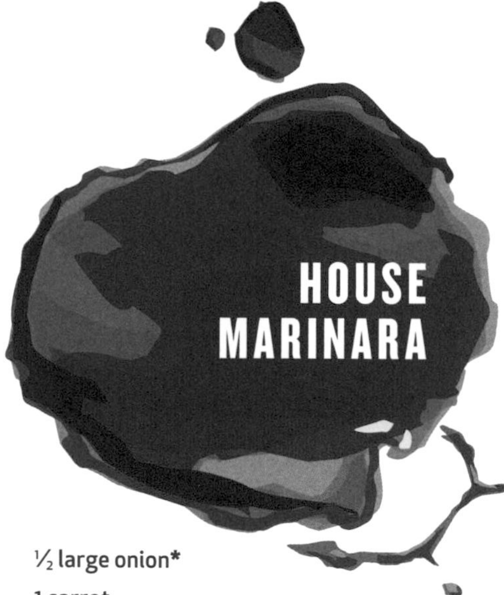

HOUSE MARINARA

Your ass should know how to make a basic marinara. It's fucking required by the laws of this book.

MAKES ABOUT 4 CUPS

½ large onion*
1 carrot
3 cloves garlic**
1 teaspoon olive oil
1 teaspoon dried thyme
Pinch of red pepper flakes
1 can (28 ounces) whole tomatoes***
Salt

* *White, yellow, or sweet will do. Whatever is on sale.*

** *Or you could use 5 cloves of roasted garlic (page 40) to mix it up.*

*** *Make sure there isn't a shit ton of salt or any other seasoning in there.*

1 Chop up the onion. Dice up the carrot into pieces about the size of a pea. Mince the garlic up small. You can do this shit in your sleep.

2 Heat the oil in a medium soup pot over medium heat. Add the onion and sauté it until begins to look golden in some places, 4 to 5 minutes. Add the carrot and cook for another 2 minutes. Add the garlic, thyme, and red pepper flakes. This should be smelling fucking choice right now.

3 Open the can of tomatoes, grab some whole tomatoes, and smash them in your fists like a fucked up stress ball. Squeeze them into a bunch of pieces and stir them into the pot as you go. Keep doing this until all the tomatoes are smashed up, then add ¾ cup of the juice from the can to the pot. Reduce the heat to medium-low and simmer this uncovered for 25 to 30 minutes, until all the tomatoes are broken down. Taste and add more garlic, thyme, salt, or whatever the fuck you think it needs.

4 If you like a smoother sauce, throw that shit in the blender or use an immersion blender to get rid of some of the chunks. The sauce will keep in the fridge for a week.

LIKE A DELICIOUS HOLE PUNCH

TOFU RICOTTA

MAKES ABOUT 2 CUPS

¼ cup raw hulled sunflower seeds
1 block (14 ounces) extra-firm tofu
1 tablespoon olive oil
½ teaspoon grated lemon zest
1 tablespoon lemon juice
¼ teaspoon salt
3 to 4 cloves garlic, minced
¼ cup nutritional yeast*

1 Pour the sunflower seeds into a food processor and run until that shit is in tiny-ass pieces.

2 Take the tofu out of its package and with your hands, squeeze out as much water as you can. Add it to the food processor and run it until it is all mixed in with the sunflower seeds and looks kinda smooth.

3 Dump that into a bowl with the olive oil, lemon zest, lemon juice, salt, and garlic. Mix that all together and then stir in the nutritional yeast. Done and done. Throw that in the fridge until you need it. You can make this shit a day ahead of time if you're pressed for time.

* *WTF? See page 10.*

MIXED MUSHROOM AND SPINACH LASAGNA

This shit is a little complicated but well worth it. Make it when you've got people to impress or when you're really fucking lonely. Real talk: This lasagna is better than friends.

MAKES ENOUGH FOR 6 TO 8 PEOPLE AT ONCE OR YOUR SINGLE ASS FOR A WEEK AND A HALF

BASIL PESTO

⅓ cup slivered or sliced almonds
1¼ cups packed torn basil leaves
2 tablespoons olive oil
2 tablespoons water
1 tablespoon lemon juice
½ teaspoon grated lemon zest
½ teaspoon salt
2 to 3 cloves garlic, chopped

MUSHROOM SPINACH FILLING

16 ounces button or cremini mushrooms*
1 teaspoon olive oil
6 cups spinach
Salt

1 pound lasagna noodles
Double batch of House Marinara (page 148)
Double batch of Tofu Ricotta (page 149)
Sliced tomatoes (optional)

* *You can do half and half or whatever.*

1 Put all the ingredients for the pesto in a food processor and blend until smooth-ish. No food processor? Chill the fuck out. Just put the almonds in a plastic bag and smash them up with a rolling pin or a can until they are tiny, and chop the rest of that shit up super small, too. Mix it with a fork until it looks like a paste. Set it aside.

2 To make the filling, remove any tough mushroom stems and slice up the mushrooms into pieces no larger than a nickel. Heat the oil in a large sauté pan over medium heat. Add the mushrooms and sauté for about 2 minutes. Fold in the spinach, add a small pinch of salt, and continue cooking until all the spinach is wilted, about 3 more minutes. Turn off the heat and stir in 2 tablespoons of the pesto. Taste and add more if you like. You know how you do.

3 Heat your oven to 375°F. Grab an 8 x 10-inch baking dish.

4 Cook the noodles according to the package directions. Ladle about 1 cup of the marinara sauce into the bottom of the baking dish and lay down enough noodles to cover the bottom with just a bit of overlap. Spread about one-third of the ricotta down, followed by one-third of the mushroom filling, and then pour another cup of the sauce over top. Spread a spoonful or two of the pesto over all of that and then do another layer of noodles. Repeat the whole process until you run out of room and top with the final layer of noodles. Cover the noodles with the remaining sauce. If you want to look extra fucking fancy, add sliced tomato rounds on top.

5 Cover that whole heavy motherfucker with foil and throw it in the oven for about 30 minutes. Gently take off the foil after that and bake it until the edges of the noodles start to look a little golden, another 25 to 30 minutes. Let it sit for 10 to 15 minutes before going to town. Top with some of the remaining pesto and serve.

GIVE THE DELIVERY
GUY A FUCKING BREAK

VEGETABLE PAD THAI WITH DRY-FRIED TOFU

Quit fucking with that tired-ass take-out. You can make better shit at home in no time. Plus, you don't have to put on pants to answer the door.

MAKES ENOUGH FOR 4

SAUCE

¼ cup lime juice
¼ cup soy sauce or tamari*
3 tablespoons water
3 tablespoons brown sugar
3 tablespoons tomato paste
3 tablespoons rice vinegar

NOODLES

14 ounces rice noodles
1 medium crown of broccoli
⅓ cup sliced shallots**
4 cloves garlic, minced
1 cup sliced green onions
¼ cup roughly chopped cilantro
2 teaspoons neutral-tasting oil***
Dry-Fried Tofu (page 154)

TOPPINGS

2 cups thinly sliced cabbage****
1 carrot, thinly sliced into matchsticks
1 cup bean sprouts
Chopped peanuts
Lime wedges

1 Mix together all the stuff for the sauce in a medium glass.

2 Cook your noodles according to the package directions. Rinse with cold water. Chop up the broccoli into pieces no bigger than a quarter and get all the rest of your veggies and herbs on lock. Get ready to stir-fry.

3 Now that you've got everything lined up, heat the oil over medium heat in a big skillet or wok. When the pan is hot, add the shallots and stir-fry those fuckers until they start to char around the edges, about 2 minutes. Add the broccoli and keep that shit up for another 2 minutes until the broccoli is kinda charred but isn't limp as fuck. Now add the garlic and fry it up for another 30 seconds. Gently add the noodles and ⅓ cup of the sauce and toss that shit all around to make sure everything is covered. Keep stirring and fold in the tofu. Cook for another 30 seconds to a minute to make sure the sauce is nice and absorbed. Keep adding more tablespoons of sauce until it is exactly how you like it. Turn off the heat and fold in the green onions and cilantro.

4 Serve this mound of deliciousness right away piled high on a plate next to the cabbages, carrots, bean sprouts, and topped with the peanuts. Have some limes wedges shoved in there and squeeze that shit over it before you dig in.

* *Don't eat this all at once because that is too much goddamn salt for one day. Fuck.*

** *Use a yellow onion if that is what you can find.*

*** *Like safflower or grapeseed*

**** *Red, green, whatthefuckever*

DRY-FRIED TOFU

Want crispy, fried tofu, without all the fucking oil? YOU GOT IT.

ENOUGH FOR 2 TO 4 PEOPLE OR TO ADD TO ONE ENTRÉE RECIPE

- **1 block extra-firm tofu, pressed for at least 30 minutes (see How to Bake Tofu, page 76)**
- **Pinch of salt**

1 Cut the tofu vertically into planks about ¼ inch thick and then cut those planks in half widthwise. You should end up with around 20 squarish pieces.

2 Preheat a large wok or cast-iron skillet* over medium heat. Once the pan is hot, add the tofu in a single layer. You might have to do this in two batches depending on the size of your pan. You'll want the tofu to sizzle once it hits the pan so if that shit is quiet, turn up the heat a little.

3 Sprinkle a pinch of salt over the tofu and start gently pressing down on the tofu with your spatula. You'll hear the steam escape from under the tofu as you do this. It sounds like screams, but keep the fuck on. Don't try and flip it yet; you got to let that shit get toasted. After 3 to 4 minutes, the bottom sides should look golden brown. Flip them over and repeat. When the tofu is cooked all over, you can cut it into strips, triangles, or smaller squares, whateverthe-fuck you like in your food. It's just easier to keep that shit bigger for flipping purposes.

* *You want a really well-seasoned pan here so that the tofu doesn't stick. If all else fails, grab a nonstick pan.*

SHOW TOFU THAT YOU DON'T
TAKE SHIT
FROM NO BEAN

SWEET POTATO, SQUASH, AND BLACK BEAN ENCHILADAS

There are two kinds of people in this world: people who like enchiladas and people who have no fucking taste. Which are you?

MAKES 8 ENCHILADAS OR ENOUGH FOR 4 PEOPLE

ENCHILADA SAUCE

2¼ cups vegetable broth
⅓ cup tomato paste
2½ tablespoons chili powder
2 teaspoons ground cumin
1½ teaspoons dried oregano
2 to 3 cloves garlic, minced
2 teaspoons soy sauce or tamari
1 tablespoon lime juice

FILLING

1 large sweet potato (about 1 pound), chopped into nickel-size pieces*
2 teaspoons olive oil
½ yellow onion, chopped
1 medium yellow squash, grated on your box grater (about 1 cup)
1 teaspoon chili powder
½ teaspoon ground cumin
½ teaspoon salt

1 Make the enchilada sauce: Dump everything but the lime juice into a medium saucepan and bring to a simmer. Use a whisk or something and make sure that the tomato paste isn't just sitting in a fucking clump. Let that simmer together for 10 to 15 minutes so that the sauce has time to thicken up a little. Add the lime juice and turn off the heat. Let that shit cool while you make the filling.

2 To cook the sweet potato, grab a medium saucepan, fill it with an inch or two of water, and bring to a boil over medium heat. Throw in your metal steamer basket and fill that with the chopped sweet potato. Cover and steam until tender, 10 to 15 minutes. Dump into a bowl and smash the pieces around. Some chunks are fine, so you don't need to work too hard at making this smooth.

3 While the sweet potato steams, grab a large skillet or wok and heat the oil over medium heat. Add the onion and sauté until it begins to brown, 3 to 5 minutes. Toss in the squash and cook for another minute. Add the chili powder, cumin, salt, garlic, and black beans. Cook together for another 2 minutes and then fold in the mashed sweet potato and maple syrup and turn off the heat. Mix until all that shit is combined.

4 Now you're going to make the motherfucking enchiladas. Crank your oven to 375°F. Grab a 9 x 13-inch baking dish.

(keep going 'cause you know we aren't done . . .)

** You really just need 1 large cooked sweet potato. If you have a leftover roasted sweet potato or something, just scoop out the flesh and move on with the recipe. Or steam it in the microwave if that is your shit: Stab it with a fork, then cook on high for 5 minutes, flip, then 5 minutes more.*

2 cloves garlic, minced
1½ cups cooked black beans**
1 teaspoon maple syrup or agave syrup
A pack of corn or flour tortillas
Sliced avocado
Chopped fresh cilantro

5 Cover the bottom of the baking dish with about 1½ cups of enchilada sauce. Using a griddle, your oven, or the microwave, warm up the tortillas. Dip a tortilla around in a little of the sauce in the baking dish so that the bottom is all coated. Fill the tortilla with a couple spoonfuls of filling, then roll it up and set it seam-side down in the dish. You know how the fuck enchiladas are supposed to look, so handle that shit. Keep going until you run out of space or out of filling.

6 Cover the enchiladas with the remaining sauce, cover the dish tightly with foil, and throw it in the oven for 20 minutes. Take off the foil and cook it for 5 more minutes. Let it cool for a minute or two before serving. Feel free to top those savory sons of bitches with some sliced avocado or chopped cilantro if you give a shit about presentation.

** *Or one 15-ounce can*

MANGO CURRY

Right by the beach in San Diego there's this dope Thai place with a mango curry that blows our fucking minds. This recipe is our attempt to keep up, but if you ever find yourself down that way, check out Thai Village for the real fucking deal.

MAKES ENOUGH FOR 4

- **1 teaspoon coconut or grapeseed oil**
- **½ onion, chopped**
- **1½ cups green beans cut into 1-inch pieces**
- **1 medium zucchini, cut into ⅛-inch half-moons**
- **1 red or yellow bell pepper, chopped**
- **3 cloves garlic, minced**
- **1½ tablespoons minced fresh ginger**
- **2 tablespoons red curry paste***
- **1 tablespoon soy sauce or tamari**
- **1½ cups canned coconut milk**
- **1 cup vegetable broth**
- **1 ripe mango, cut into chunks (see page 74)**
- **Dry-Fried Tofu (page 154)**
- **2 tablespoons lime juice**
- **Basic Big Pot of Brown Rice (page xxiv)**

1 Grab a medium soup pot and heat the oil over a medium heat. Add the onion and sauté until lightly golden, about 3 minutes. Add the green beans, zucchini, and bell pepper and cook until the vegetables begin to soften up, another 2 to 3 minutes. Add the garlic, ginger, and curry paste and cook for another 30 seconds. Huff in that goddamn delicious smell. Add the soy sauce, coconut milk, and vegetable broth and turn that son of a bitch to a gentle simmer.

2 Once the pot is gently simmering, add the mango and tofu. Reduce the heat to low and let this all cook together until the mango is tender enough to fall apart, 5 to 8 minutes. Turn off the heat, add the lime juice, and then dish up. Serve over the brown rice and tell your neighbors to fucking go home when they stop by asking what smells so good.

** You can find this in a glass jar or small can shelved near the coconut milk and soy sauces. It's made of all kinds of shit like shallots, lemongrass, galangal, and red chiles. Some pastes are hotter than others, so try 1 tablespoon first and then work your way up in the recipe. There are hundreds of recipes for making this shit yourself, so if you have a well-stocked store, look a recipe up and make this fucker from scratch. The hardest part is finding all the ingredients, trust.*

DROPPING KNOWLEDGE

USDA ORGANIC

WHAT THE FUCK DOES ORGANIC MEAN?

When it comes to marketing, food companies pull all kinds of nonsense to sell consumers their bullshit. You need to know the definition of these "green" terms to keep from getting fucked when you shop.

Here's the deal: organic foods are grown and produced without using conventional pesticides, synthetic fertilizers, sewage sludge, irradiation, or genetic engineering. Before products can be labeled organic, a third-party certifier inspects the farm annually to make sure all the United States Department of Agriculture's (USDA) organic standards are being met. All that shit costs money, so that's one reason why organic food tends to cost more. And while some small farms may grow all their grub organically, they may not be able to afford the certification. Know that shit. Salt and water can't be labeled organic, so if you see someone claiming their water is organic, slap it out of their hand and laugh in their face. Here's a breakdown of the green name game:

100 Percent Organic: This product or produce was found by a third party to contain only organic ingredients. Look for the USDA seal to know that shit is legit.

Organic: This is 95 percent organic and that other 5 percent of stuff can only be items from a list of USDA-approved ingredients. The USDA seal will cover this, too.

Made with Organic Ingredients: This means the product contains at least 70 percent organic ingredients. That stuff will be marked with an asterisk on the ingredients list.

Natural: This shit signifies nothing when it comes to fruits, vegetables, grains, and legumes. You can throw this word on anything to make it seem healthy or environmentally friendly and it doesn't mean jack shit because it is totally unregulated.

Also, watch for assholes who use organic in their product or company name to confuse the fuck out of people. Take a damn second and read labels carefully so you don't get played by these bitches.

SILKY ROASTED BELL PEPPER PASTA WITH ZUCCHINI AND BASIL RIBBONS

Don't let a little soybean scare your ass off this sexy summer meal. This is dope with the Almond Caesar Salad (page 39) if you are trying to serve courses and shit with your dinner.

MAKES ENOUGH FOR 4 AS A MAIN DISH, BUT IF YOU'RE SOLO THESE LEFTOVERS ARE LEGIT ENOUGH TO HOLD YOU OVER FOR THE BETTER PART OF A WEEK

SILKY RED PEPPER SAUCE

12 ounces soft silken tofu*
2 roasted red bell peppers (opposite), chopped
3 to 4 cloves garlic, minced
1½ tablespoons red wine vinegar
2 teaspoons olive oil
¼ cup nutritional yeast**
¾ teaspoon salt
1 teaspoon red pepper flakes

PASTA

1 pound spaghetti, linguine, or fettuccine***
4 medium zucchini****
1 cup basil, sliced into thin strips

1 First make the sauce. Throw everything together in a blender or a food processor and run on high until the sauce is smooth. Pour it into a small saucepan and stick it on the stove. We'll come back to this shit in a minute.

2 Now cook the pasta according to the package directions . . . or your pasta instincts. While the pasta is cooking, slice the zucchini into thin matchsticks. Yeah, show off those knife skills. Try to get the strips as close as you can to the size of the noodles so they can blend in when you mix those motherfuckers together. Don't spend all day trying to make this happen. Just aim for noodle twins and fucking deal with wherever you end up.

3 Right before the pasta is done, start up a low heat under the sauce you made earlier so it warms up, but doesn't simmer. When the pasta is done, drain it, and then immediately throw it in a large bowl. Add the zucchini ribbons to the hot pasta and then add the warmed-up sauce. Mix it all around and the heat from the pasta and sauce should start to soften the zucchini just a little bit. Fold in the basil and then taste. Add more vinegar, salt, or red pepper flakes—whatever you feel like. Top with a basil leaf or two and serve right away.

* *You want the kind in aseptic packaging. It's on the shelf near the soy sauce.*

** *WTF? See page 10.*

*** *Whole wheat or regular pasta will do. Just use long, thin noodles.*

**** *Aim for zucchini 4 to 5 inches long, with the circumference of a baby's arm.*

HOW TO ROAST YOUR OWN BELL PEPPERS

Stop buying roasted bell peppers in a jar like an asshole. Just light your money on fire if you don't give a fuck. This shit is super easy to do and will save you money. Grab some foil, peppers, and get your ass to the stove.

1. Place each bell pepper on the center of a burner of a gas stove* and turn the heat to high. Burn the shit out of the skin of each pepper, rotating it until every side has blackened. Make sure to use tongs or something—*not* your hands—or be prepared to live with the consequences of your dumbass decision.
2. When the peppers are burnt all the way around, place each one in a piece of foil and wrap it up tight so that no steam escapes. Let them cool for like 15 minutes.
3. When the peppers have cooled, the burnt skin will be a little separated from the flesh of the pepper and you should be able to peel that shit off no problem. Don't run the pepper under the tap thinking you are saving time. You will lose the awesome roasted flavor, so don't fuck things up now.

Once you've peeled the peppers, go make something badass like the Silky Roasted Bell Pepper Pasta on the opposite page or throw it in some House Marinara (page 148). You can do this shit a day or two in advance; just keep them in the fridge in an airtight container.

*****_If you are working with an electric stove, you aren't getting left out. Just heat up your oven to 400°F and line a baking sheet with some foil. Lay your peppers down on there, roast them for 25 minutes, turn, and roast them for 25 more until they look all charred and soft. Wrap them up in foil just like the stovetop ones and follow the rest of the steps. Done and fucking done._

IT CAME FROM THE GROUND

IN TRU-STEREO 3DIMENSION!

NO KITCHEN ON EARTH COULD CONTAIN...

THE BIG-ASS CAULIFLOWER

CAULIFLOWER CREAM PASTA WITH FRESH HERBS

Want to enjoy creamy pasta without having to fucking worry about your cholesterol? Pureed cauliflower makes this sauce silky without any of that added bullshit that made you avoid creamy sauces for so long. Feel free to add some stuff like roasted asparagus, steamed broccoli, or roasted red peppers to this dish to mix it up.

MAKES ENOUGH FOR 4

- 1 pound pasta (fettuccine, linguine, spaghetti, whatever)
- 4 cups chopped spinach
- Salt and pepper
- ½ head cauliflower (about 1 pound), cut into little trees
- ½ cup unsweetened plain nondairy milk
- 2 or 3 cloves garlic, minced
- 1 tablespoon lemon juice
- 1 tablespoon olive oil
- 1 teaspoon miso paste*
- ⅓ cup minced fresh parsley

1 Cook the pasta according to the package directions or whatever fucking method you invented and now swear by. When it's all done, throw it in a large bowl with the spinach, toss, and set aside.

2 While the pasta cooks, bring a medium pot of water to a boil. Throw in a pinch of salt and the cauliflower and simmer all that until the cauliflower is tender, 5 to 7 minutes. Drain the cauliflower and toss into a blender.

3 Add the milk, garlic, lemon juice, olive oil, miso, and ⅛ teaspoon salt to the blender and let that motherfucker run until the sauce is creamy. Taste and adjust as you see fit.

4 Pour the cauliflower puree into the pot you boiled the cauliflower in and set over low heat. Add the pasta and spinach and toss until everything is mixed and warm. Top with some parsley and salt and pepper to taste. Serve hot.

* *Whatever you bought to make soup will work here. WTF? See page 88.*

ROASTED CHICKPEA AND BROCCOLI BURRITOS

This is a fan favorite that had to appear in the book. It's a weeknight staple and one bad burrito you deserve to have in your life. Listen to the fans. They know what's up.

MAKES 4 TO 6 BURRITOS

GRUB LIKE A
CHAMP
NOT LIKE A
CHUMP

CHICKPEAS AND GARBANZO BEANS ARE THE SAME FUCKING THING

YOU'RE WELCOME

1 Crank your oven to 425°F. Grab a large rimmed baking sheet.

2 Chop up the onion, bell pepper, and broccoli 'til they're the size of a chickpea. Place all the chopped up veggies in a large bowl with the cooked chickpeas. Pour in the oil and soy sauce, stir, and then throw all the spices in there. Mix until all the vegetables and shit are covered. Put all of that on the baking sheet and bake for 20 minutes.

3 Take it out of the oven—don't fucking burn yourself—then add the garlic and stir it around. Bake for another 15 minutes. The broccoli might look a little burnt at this point but that is the plan, so chill the fuck out and take it out of the oven. Squeeze the lime juice over the pan and stir the roasted chickpeas and veggies all around. Taste and see if it needs more spices or anything.

4 Now make a motherfucking burrito. We like ours with spinach, avocado, cilantro, and some fire-roasted salsa, but do your thing.

* *Or two 15-ounce cans*

** *WTF? See page 10.*

*** *Or more cumin if you don't want to go to the store.*

1 large yellow onion
1 red bell pepper
1 large crown of broccoli
3 cups cooked chickpeas*
3 tablespoons olive oil
1 to 2 tablespoons soy sauce, tamari, or Bragg's**
2 teaspoons chili powder
1 teaspoon ground cumin
1 teaspoon smoked paprika
½ teaspoon ground coriander***
Cayenne pepper, to taste
4 cloves garlic, minced
½ lime
4 to 6 flour tortillas
Burrito trimmings such as spinach, avocado, cilantro, and Fire-Roasted Salsa (page 124)

ROASTED BEER AND LIME CAULIFLOWER TACOS WITH CILANTRO COLESLAW

Grab beer and get to work. Just don't get sloppy 'til you're done cooking.

MAKES ABOUT 6 TACOS

- 1 head cauliflower (about 1 pound)
- ¾ cup beer*
- ¼ cup vegetable broth**
- 1 tablespoon lime juice
- 1½ teaspoons soy sauce or tamari
- 1½ tablespoons of your go-to chipotle hot sauce
- 1 to 2 cloves garlic, sliced
- 1½ teaspoons chili powder
- 1 teaspoon smoked paprika
- ¼ teaspoon ground cumin
- ¼ teaspoon garlic powder
- Pinch of salt
- 1 tablespoon olive oil
- ½ yellow onion, chopped
- 6 corn tortillas
- 1 avocado, sliced
- Quick Lime and Cilantro Slaw (page 168)
- Fire-Roasted Salsa (page 124)

1 Crank your oven to 400°F. Grab a rimmed baking sheet.

2 Chop the cauliflower into small florets no bigger than a quarter. In a saucepan, warm the beer, broth, lime juice, tamari, hot sauce, and garlic over medium heat. Add the cauliflower and simmer for about 1½ minutes. Drain.

3 Toss the spices, salt, and olive oil together in a large bowl. Add the cauliflower and onion and stir 'til those fuckers are coated. Dump it on the baking sheet and bake until browned, stirring halfway, about 20 minutes.

4 To make the tacos, warm the tortillas in the oven or microwave for a hot minute and then pile them high with the cauliflower filling, slices of avocado, some of the slaw, and top with plenty of salsa.

* *Whatever you are cool with drinking the rest of is fine here. Just no coffee stout or anything heavy like that.*

** *For homemade shit, go to page 86, but use what you got.*

CORN·VE·LOPE
A CORN TORTILLA FOLDED UP TO DELIVER TASTY TACO MAIL DIRECTLY TO YOUR TASTE BUDS. THESE ROASTED CAULIFLOWER TACOS ARE A SPECIAL FUCKING DELIVERY
FUCK YEAH

QUICK LIME AND CILANTRO SLAW

This fucker is great in any taco, any time. Memorize this shit because you won't be going back to empty tacos again.

- ½ head of green cabbage (about ½ pound)
- 1 small carrot
- 2 tablespoons lime juice
- 2 tablespoons rice vinegar
- 1 teaspoon olive oil
- ⅛ teaspoon salt
- ⅓ cup chopped cilantro

Cut the cabbage into the thinnest strips you can and make sure those pieces are no longer than 2 inches. This is a great time to get good with your knife if you are looking for a silver fucking lining in all that chopping. Chop the carrot into thin matchsticks of the same length. Got that shit down now, right? In a small glass, mix together the lime juice, vinegar, oil, and salt. Add the dressing right before you are going to eat and toss that shit well. Add the cilantro and serve.

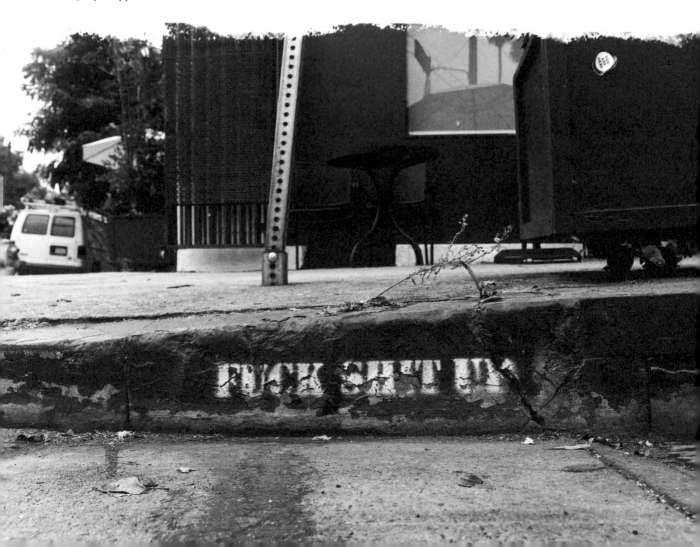

TEMPEH PEANUT NOODLES WITH BLANCHED KALE

These noodles make for legit leftovers. First night, eat them straight. For lunch the next day, add some carrot and cucumber that you cut into matchsticks, and eat it cold like a salad. It's a lazy costume change but nobody will fucking notice.

MAKES ENOUGH FOR 4

PEANUT SAUCE

½ cup creamy peanut butter*

½ cup warm water

¼ cup rice vinegar

2 teaspoons toasted sesame oil

2 teaspoons lime juice

2 teaspoons soy sauce or tamari

1 teaspoon maple syrup or agave syrup

1 teaspoon chili-garlic paste or Asian-style hot sauce (optional**)

NOODLES AND VEGGIES

12 ounces noodles***

6 cups kale, sliced into bite-size pieces

1 teaspoon grapeseed or refined coconut oil

8 ounces tempeh

1 teaspoon soy sauce or tamari

1 tablespoon rice vinegar

2 tablespoons minced fresh ginger

3 cloves garlic, minced

½ cup sliced green onions

1 First make the peanut sauce. In a medium glass, whisk together the peanut butter and water until it looks all creamy. Add all the other ingredients and keep stirring until everything is incorporated. Simple shit.

2 Now cook the noodles according to the package directions, but use a larger soup pot than usual. In the last 30 seconds of cooking the noodles, add the kale to the pot and stir it into the water to make sure it's all covered. After 30 seconds, drain the pasta and kale and run it under cold water to stop the cooking process and keep the kale green. That's called lazy-ass blanching. Some people might say to do that shit in separate pots, but those are usually the motherfuckers who don't wash their own dishes, so fuck them.

3 Grab a big wok or skillet and heat up the oil. Crumble in the tempeh in bite-size pieces and sauté it around until it starts to brown, 2 to 3 minutes. Add the soy sauce, vinegar, ginger, and garlic and cook it for 30 seconds more. Turn off the heat and add the noodles and three-quarters of the peanut sauce. Mix it all up to make sure everything is covered and that the tempeh is blended into the noodles. Taste it and if it isn't saucy enough for you, add the rest of the sauce now. Otherwise, hold on to that shit because the noodles really absorb the sauce as they sit, so it's nice to have extra for leftovers. Top with the green onions and serve warm or at room temperature.

* *Don't buy peanut butter that has anything other than peanuts, a little oil, and salt listed as ingredients. Anything else is unfuckingnecessary.*

** *Optional, but you should suck it up and do it.*

*** *Soba, udon, spaghetti, whatthefuckever.*

WHITE BEAN AND RED LENTIL BURGERS

This isn't one of those flavorless fauxmeat burgers you might see at restaurants. This is a veggie burger with a bite that will have you making a second batch in no time flat. It goes great with a side of Root Veggie Fries (opposite) or some Roasted Potato Salad (page 45).

MAKES 8 LARGE BURGER PATTIES

- **⅓ cup red lentils**
- **⅔ cup water**
- **3 cups cooked white beans**
- **½ red onion, chopped**
- **3 cloves garlic, minced**
- **1 jalapeño, minced**
- **½ cup breadcrumbs**
- **1½ teaspoons smoked paprika**
- **1½ teaspoons of your favorite no-salt, all-purpose seasoning blend**
- **1 teaspoon ground cumin**
- **1 tablespoon olive oil**
- **½ teaspoon salt**
- **Grated zest of ½ lime**
- **Cooking spray**
- **Burger fixings, like buns, lettuce, tomato, onions, etc.**

1 Combine the lentils and water in a medium saucepan and bring to a boil. Reduce the heat and let that all simmer until the lentils are soft and mushy and the water is mostly gone, about 10 minutes. Drain away any extra water and let the lentils cool while you prep all the other shit.

2 Mash the white beans in a large bowl and then add the lentils and the rest of the ingredients (not counting the cooking spray and fixings). If you find the mixture too wet to hold its shape, add some more breadcrumbs. Shape that mix into patties (you know, burger size) and put them on an oiled baking sheet. Chill that in the fridge, covered, for at least 30 minutes or up to 4 hours.

3 Crank your oven to 400°F when you're ready to go. Coat the patties lightly with some cooking spray and bake them for about 30 minutes, flipping them over halfway. You want them to be golden on both sides. Serve them up with whatever the fuck you like on a burger and then go to town.

ROOT VEGGIE FRIES

Crank your oven to 425°F. Line a rimmed baking sheet with parchment paper or foil. Mix together the flour, spices, and salt in a small bowl. Toss together the lemon juice, soy sauce, and olive oil in a large bowl and add the root veggies. Sprinkle the spice mixture over the roots and mix until everything is all well coated. Spread the roots over the baking sheet and bake until the fries are golden and slightly crispy, about 30 minutes, turning halfway through. Serve warm with your favorite dipping sauce.

5 tablespoons brown rice flour or white flour
½ teaspoon garlic powder
½ teaspoon chili powder
⅛ teaspoon salt
1 tablespoon lemon juice
1 teaspoon soy sauce or tamari
2 tablespoons olive oil
2 pounds of whatever root veggies you can find, peeled and cut into matchsticks no larger than a finger*

* *Fry size, for any of you dense motherfuckers out there. You can grab potatoes, carrots, parsnips, turnips—whatever mix you like.*

TRY NEW THINGS
START WITH FRIES

BBQ BEAN BURRITOS WITH GRILLED PEACH SALSA

This burrito is loosely based on something you used to be able to grab at LA's famed Pure Luck restaurant. It broke some hearts when that motherfucker closed, but at least this dope dish was born out of our withdrawals. RIP Pure Luck.

MAKES 6 BIG-ASS BURRITOS

BBQ BEANS

½ yellow or white onion, chopped
3 tablespoons tomato paste
3 to 4 cloves garlic, minced
4 chipotle peppers in adobo sauce* plus 1 tablespoon of the sauce
¼ cup vegetable broth or water
2 tablespoons orange juice
2 tablespoons light brown sugar
1 tablespoon molasses
1 teaspoon soy sauce or tamari
3 cups cooked pinto beans**

BURRITO STUFF

6 burrito-size flour tortillas
Baked Spanish Rice (page 81)
Shredded lettuce
Grilled Peach Salsa (page 123)
Sliced avocado

1 First, make the BBQ beans: Throw the onion, tomato paste, garlic, chipotle peppers and sauce, broth, OJ, brown sugar, molasses, and soy sauce in a food processor or blender and run that fucker until a smooth sauce forms. Pour that into a medium saucepan over medium-low heat, fold in the beans, and simmer until everything is warm and the beans absorb all that flavor, 5 to 10 minutes.

2 To make the burritos: Grab your tortilla and pile in a scoop of the beans, some rice, and a handful of lettuce and top with the peach salsa and some avocado. Serve right away because burritos wait for no motherfucker.

* *These smoked peppers come packed in sauce and are sold in a tiny can at most stores near the salsa and beans. Trust us, it's there, just fucking look before you start whining.*

** *Two 15-ounce cans if you aren't cooking this shit yourself*

HOT
DAMN

HOW TO BUILD A BOWL

One of the easier ways to make dinner filling as fuck and mix up your familiar flavor combos is to build a bowl. Just pile a bunch of shit into a bowl and dig in. It's also a great way to eat up any leftovers without feeling like you have been eating the same shit every day all week. Bowls are the answer and we're going to show you the way.

1. Begin with a grain or some starch to take up about one-third of the bowl. This could be some kind of rice, noodles, couscous, quinoa, potatoes . . . just something substantial to serve as the base.
2. Next you need some veggies to fill up at least another third to half of the bowl. This can be as simple as sautéed greens and shredded carrots, or you can go for broke and grill up a bunch of seasonal veggies like in the Spring Veggie Bowl (page 177). You just want to make sure that you are getting a good amount and a little variety. When in doubt, just grab some fucking kale and move on.
3. Now you need some protein to fill up the rest of that bowl space. This can be some cooked beans, baked tofu, tempeh, whateverthefuck you are craving or have left over in the fridge. Just make sure your flavor combos make some goddamn sense. Throwing together a bowl of mint-flavored quinoa with Apple Baked Beans (page 67) as the protein would be gnarly. So don't do that shit. Trust your gut and your bowl will be golden.
4. Lastly, a lot of people pile on a sauce or dressing of some kind at the end—like in the breakfast Brown Rice Bowl (page 11)—to tie it all together. That is a fucking awesome choice if you are using simple ingredients that need a punch of flavor. But if you have a super saucy protein, just skip that step.

Still don't know where to start? Here are some combos from shit in this book to get you going:

S Lemon-Mint Quinoa (page 44); V shredded lettuce, carrots, and cucumbers; and the P chickpea filling from Spiced Chickpea Wraps with Tahini Dressing (page 32)

S Basic Big Pot of Brown Rice (page xxiv) or Roasted Potato Salad with Fresh Herbs (page 45); V Wilted Greens (page 80) and the savory tempeh from P Savory Tempeh and Carrot Sandwiches (page 55) topped with tahini dressing from Spiced Chickpea Wraps (page 32)

S Cooked quinoa (page xxiii); V shredded lettuce, carrots, and cucumbers; Roasted Sriracha Cauliflower Bites with Peanut Dipping Sauce (page 128); and P Dry-Fried Tofu (page 154)

S Baked Spanish Rice (page 81); V shredded kale; Grilled Peach Salsa (page 123); and the pinto beans from P BBQ Bean Burritos (page 172)

S Cooked rice noodles (see Vietnamese Rice Noodle Salad, page 50); V shredded greens, carrots, and Quick Pickled Cucumbers and Onions (page 120); and P Sweet Citrus Baked Tofu (page 77) and Sweet Fresh Herb Salsa (page 124)

S Basic Big Pot of Brown Rice (page xxiv); V Braised Winter Cabbage and Potatoes (page 48); and P Apple Baked Beans (page 67)

SPRING VEGGIE BOWL
WITH RED CURRY LIME SAUCE

Saucey and smokey, this layered son of a bitch is good hot or cold. Don't let spring pass by without making a big-ass bowl of this.

MAKES 4 TO 6 BOWLS THAT WILL LEAVE YOU FULL AS FUCK

8 ounces thin rice noodles

Red Curry Lime Sauce (page 178)

4 heads baby bok choy, halved lengthwise

2 tablespoons grapeseed oil, plus more for grilling

1 pound asparagus, trimmed

½ lime

Salt

Ginger-Sesame or Sweet Citrus Baked Tofu (page 77), cut into strips

½ cup sliced green onions

1 Cook the noodles according to the package directions. When they're all done, drain them, run them under cool water for a sec, and then set them aside. We will need these fuckers later.

2 Next, make the Red Curry Lime Sauce.

3 Brush the baby bok choy with 1 tablespoon of the oil and toss the asparagus with the other 1 tablespoon. Now heat up your grill or grill pan to medium-high and lightly grease it up with a thin layer of oil. Throw on the asparagus and grill those pointy fuckers until all the sides have some grill marks and the stalk has a little give when you pick it up with your tongs, 5 to 8 minutes with periodic rotation. Next, add the bok choy and cook on each side for 3 to 4 minutes so that they pick up some nice grill marks. When the veggies are done, squeeze the lime juice over them and add a sprinkle of salt. When the bok choy is cool enough to handle, cut each piece in half one more time from top to bottom so that shit is easier to eat. Cut the asparagus into 1-inch pieces for the same fucking reason.

4 Now throw together your bowls. Start by placing a handful of the noodles (about 1 cup) on one side of the bottom of your bowl. On the other two-thirds of the bowl, pile in a bunch of the grilled veggies and tofu strips. Drizzle the whole fucking thing with the sauce, top with the green onions, and serve right away.

RED CURRY LIME SAUCE

This sauce is great to keep in the fridge for when your leftovers are tasting a little blah.

- 1 cup vegetable broth
- 2 tablespoons red curry paste*
- ½ teaspoon grated lime zest
- 2 tablespoons lime juice
- 2 tablespoons minced fresh ginger
- 1 tablespoon peanut butter
- 1 tablespoon brown sugar, maple syrup, or agave syrup
- 2 teaspoons soy sauce or tamari
- 1 clove garlic, minced
- 1 tablespoon cornstarch or arrowroot powder**

1 Measure out 1 tablespoon of the vegetable broth and set it aside in a small glass.

2 Put the rest of the broth in a small saucepan and bring it to a simmer. Add the curry paste, lime zest, lime juice, ginger, peanut butter, sugar, soy sauce, and garlic. Mix it all up and make sure there aren't any curry or peanut butter chunks.

3 Mix together the cornstarch with the broth you put in the small glass until there are no more chunks. This is going to thicken up that watery-ass sauce, just wait. Pour this into the simmering sauce and whisk until the sauce starts getting nice and thick, about 1 minute. Turn off the heat, taste, and add more garlic, lime juice, or whatever your tongue is craving. Let it cool for at least a couple minutes before serving.

* *See page 158 for some more about this.*

** *Either of these will thicken the fuck out of your sauce.*

DON'T REWARD
ADORABLE BEGGING

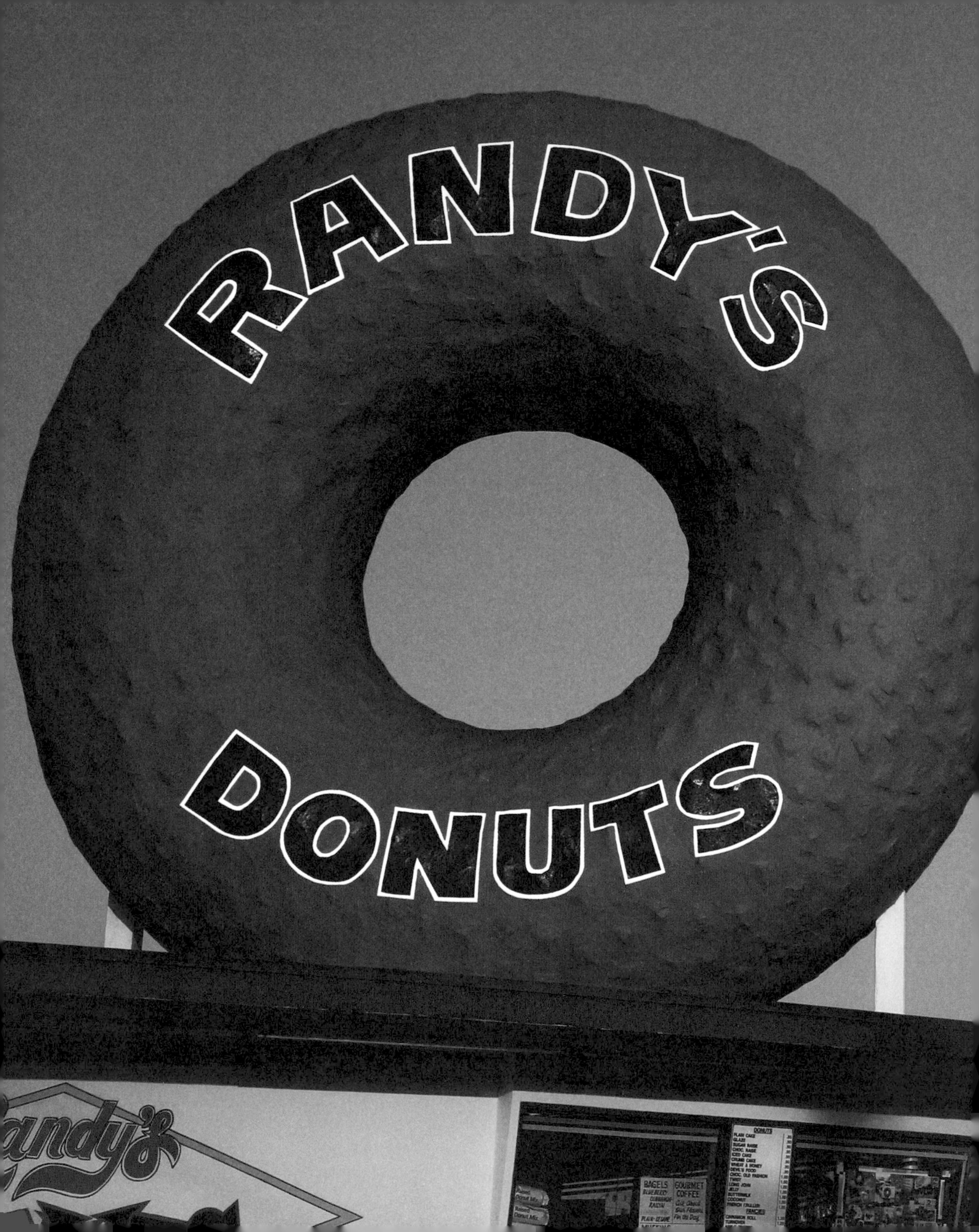

RANDY'S
DONUTS

sweet talk

BAKED GOODS AND
MOTHERFUCKING DESSERT

CHOCOLATE FUDGE POPS

Fuck the ice cream man and his unpredictable schedule. Stash these in your freezer and you can have pops on demand all summer long.

MAKES ABOUT 3⅓ CUPS FILLING, WHICH MAKES 12 POPS IN A STANDARD MOLD BUT VARIES DEPENDING ON WHATEVER FUCKING MOLD YOU USE

- 1 cup vanilla almond or your favorite nondairy milk
- 1¼ cups semisweet chocolate chips
- 12 ounces firm silken tofu*
- 12 popsicle sticks
- Popsicle molds or 12 small-ass paper cups

1 Warm up the milk on the stovetop or in the microwave so that it is warm but not super fucking hot. Next you need to melt the chocolate. You can melt it either by slowly heating it in the microwave in 25-second increments and stirring until it is melted—OR you build a double boiler like a fucking boss. Grab a medium saucepan and fill it with 1 or 2 inches of water. Throw an all-metal bowl on top of that and make sure the whole mouth of the pan is covered and that the water inside isn't touching the bottom of the bowl. Put this over medium-low heat and pour the chocolate chips into the bowl. The steam will heat the bowl and melt the chips; just keep stirring the chocolate and fucking trust the method. When the chocolate looks all smooth, turn off the heat. This whole process should take about 3 minutes.

2 Once the chocolate is melted, add it, the milk, and the tofu to a blender and mix that shit up. Make sure everything is well combined and there are no secret chocolate chunks hiding out. Pour this into your molds and stick them in the freezer for about 40 minutes. At that point, take out your pop molds and then push the sticks in. Freezing these motherfuckers a little bit first helps make sure you won't push the stick so far in that you end up with some sad-ass kabob. Freeze until hard. They will keep for at least a month in the freezer.

* *You want the shit in the aseptic packaging. The kind of package you find on the shelf near the soy sauce, not tofu packed in water in the fridge.*

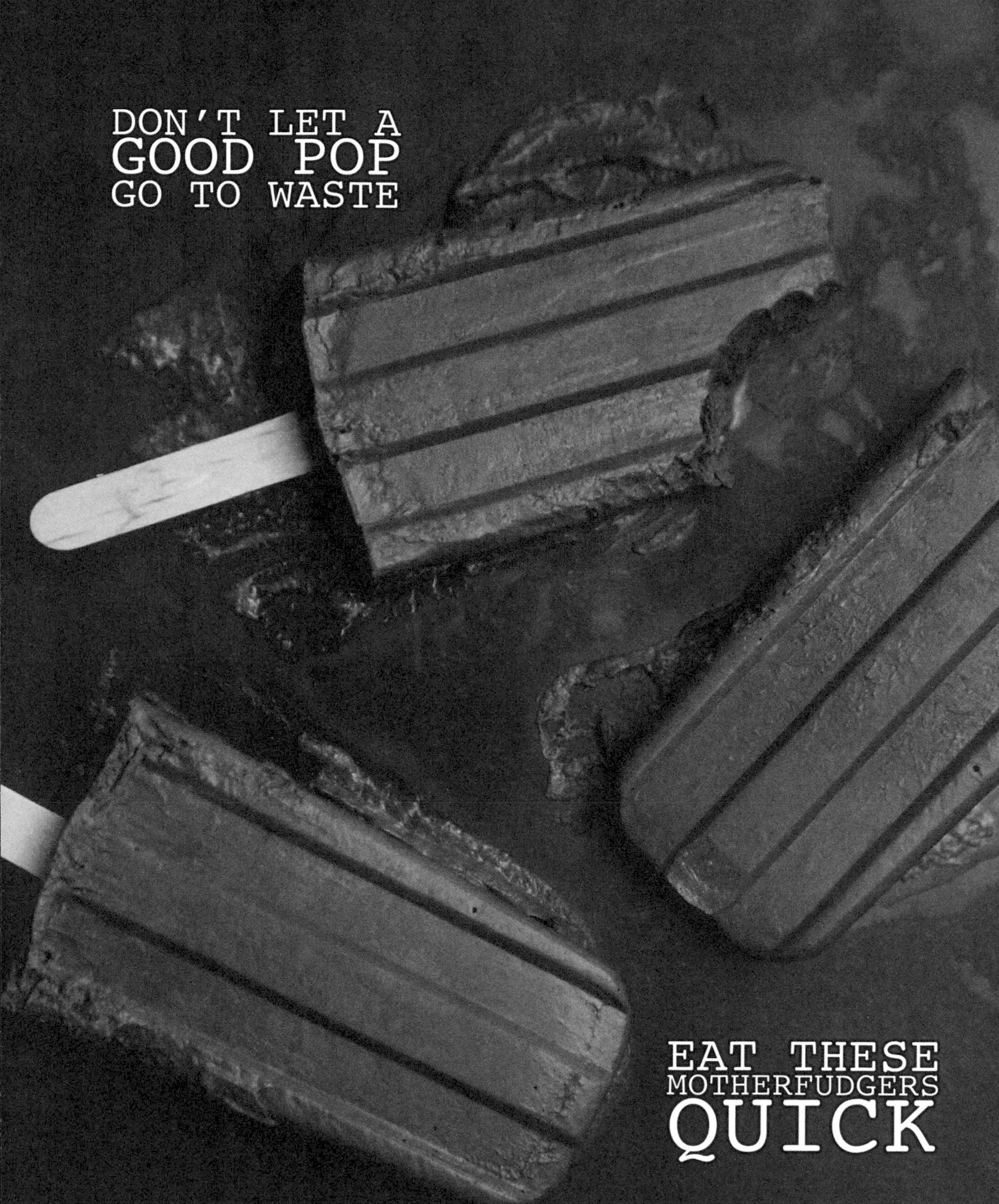

DON'T LET A
GOOD POP
GO TO WASTE
EAT THESE
MOTHERFUDGERS
QUICK

CHOCOLATE-DIPPED TANGERINES

Bust these out during the holidays and people will forget all about the presents.

MAKES ABOUT 30 SLICES, DEPENDING ON YOUR CITRUS

5 or 6 tangerines, clementines, or tiny oranges of any kind
½ cup semisweet chocolate chips
1 teaspoon coconut oil
½ teaspoon sea salt

1 Peel the fruit and break them up into segments. Try to get all that white pith off because that shit will taste bitter. Lay the segments on a baking sheet lined with wax paper in some kind of order.

2 Melt the chocolate in a double boiler or the microwave (see page 182 for how). Add the coconut oil to the chocolate chips and stir until everything is melted and mixed together. Turn off the heat.

3 Dip half a citrus segment into the melted chocolate mixture and lay it flat on the baking sheet. Repeat with remaining segments. Sprinkle the chocolate dipped ends with some sea salt to dazzle motherfuckers.

4 Place the baking sheet in a cool area and let the chocolate firm up before serving, 15 to 45 minutes depending on the temperature in your pad. You can stick this in the fridge if you are in a rush.

DROPPING KNOWLEDGE

SUGAR IS IN FUCKING EVERYTHING

You're damn right we've got a dessert section in the motherfucking book. When most people try a healthier diet, they immediately go cold turkey on the dessert, but that shit is unsustainable and you'll end up just binge-eating Sour Patch Kids until you burn off your taste buds. Don't fucking go down that road. You can still eat sugar, still have dessert, just don't do that shit every day. Besides, sugar isn't just creeping around in your desserts; that motherfucker is in everything.

The USDA estimates that since the 1950s our consumption of sweeteners has risen by 40 percent per capita. GOD. DAMN. Now that doesn't mean that everybody suddenly joined Team Cake, rather that we've started putting sugar in a bunch of foods where that shit really isn't necessary. When you buy breakfast cereals, salad dressings, pasta sauces, canned/frozen foods, and commercial breads, you're knee-deep in sugar. That's another reason you need to start cooking your own shit, because those grocery shelves can't be trusted. When you're able to control how much sugar you're getting in your diet, you don't need to feel bad about having some cookies or pie once in a while. And don't even get us fucking started on soda. That overpriced can of high fructose fuckery is just a waste of everyone's goddamn time. Drink water. Make your own food. Allow yourself to eat dessert once in a while. You'll be surprised at what a difference it makes when you take control of the ingredients in your fucking food.

CRISPY MILLET AND PEANUT BUTTER BUCKEYES

No clue what in the fuck a buckeye is? It's a tasty treat from the Midwest that is supposed to resemble an Ohio buckeye tree nut. Breaking that down even more, it's basically a peanut butter cup in ball form. Don't waste any more time trying to understand this shit, just make it.

MAKES ABOUT 24 BUCKEYES

½ teaspoon oil*
⅓ cup uncooked millet**
⅔ cup creamy peanut butter***
¼ cup powdered sugar****
2 tablespoons flour
1½ teaspoons vanilla extract
1 cup semisweet chocolate chips
1 teaspoon coconut oil, if needed

* *Olive oil, grapeseed, coconut . . . almost anything is cool here.*

** *WTF? See page xxiii*

*** *Don't buy shit that has more than 3 ingredients, OK? Bad fucking news.*

**** *Yeah, this is dessert, so relax.*

1 Heat the oil in a skillet over medium heat and toss in the millet. Shake the millet around in the pan until it starts to smell toasted and look a little golden, 3 to 5 minutes. Set it aside.

2 Line a baking sheet with parchment paper. In a medium bowl, mix together the peanut butter, powdered sugar, flour, and vanilla until a thick dough is formed. Fold in the millet and mix until that shit is all in there. Make walnut-size balls with the dough and put them on the baking sheet. You should get about 24. You can lick your fingers here, we won't snitch. Put them in the freezer for at least 30 minutes or up to 2 hours.

3 Right before you are about to take out the peanut butter balls, you need to melt that chocolate. (For an easy technique for melting chocolate, see page 182.) When the chocolate looks all smooth, turn off the heat. This whole process should take about 3 minutes.

4 Gently lower a ball into the chocolate using a fork, and spoon the chocolate over the ball to coat all the sides. Traditionally you are supposed to a leave the little spot of peanut butter open at the top, but if you find it easier to just roll all those bitches in the chocolate, don't fight it. If you're having trouble doing it, stir in the coconut oil while the chocolate is still hot and it will loosen that bastard up. Drip off the excess chocolate and place the buckeye down on the baking sheet and repeat with the rest of the balls. Freeze them on the tray for at least 3 hours before serving. Store in an airtight container and they will keep for 2 weeks in the fridge or freezer. But for real, you will eat them long before then.

DON'T THESE
TINY BASTARDS
LOOK CUTE

PEACHY ALMOND TAPIOCA PUDDING

Tapioca pudding might sound like an old lady dessert but trust them; they aren't wasting their golden years on some bush-league bullshit. This pudding is creamy and perfectly sweet. Now go call Gladys and tell her that shit Ethel said earlier.

MAKES ENOUGH FOR 4 NORMAL PEOPLE

½ cup small tapioca pearls*
2 cups water
3 cups peach juice**
1 cup plain almond milk
Pinch of salt
½ teaspoon vanilla extract
1 tablespoon agave syrup (optional)
2 tablespoons lemon juice
Blueberries, for serving

1 Put the tapioca pearls in a bowl with the water and let them soak overnight. You can do this in the morning too; they just need to sit for at least 6 hours. Don't let them go more than 16 hours, though. Shit gets weird after that.

2 When you are ready to cook, drain the tapioca pearls. Put them in a medium saucepan with the juice, almond milk, salt, and vanilla. If your juice isn't super sweet, then go ahead and add the agave. Just fucking taste it and you will figure it out. Warm the pot over low heat and stir constantly. You don't want it bubbling or anything, so pay attention and don't fucking stop stirring. At around 8 to 10 minutes it should start thickening up and the pearls should start looking clear. Keep stirring until it is about the same consistency as a thick soup or gravy, about a minute more. Turn off the heat and stir in the lemon juice. Pour the pudding into a medium bowl and put in the fridge to cool.

3 Let it sit for 3 to 4 hours, otherwise you'll be eating hot pudding and that shit is gross. If it thickens up too much in the fridge, just stir it up real good and add an extra tablespoon of peach juice. Top the tapioca with blueberries and serve.

* *These little white balls are usually sold in bags in the baking aisle of the store or just look on the Internet. They are the starch that helps this thicken up so don't even fucking think about leaving them out.*

** *You can use whatever the fuck kind of juice you want, just not something real acidic like orange. Peach-apple juice is a good one, too.*

STRAWBERRY SHORTCAKE

This dessert is an American classic because IT'S FUCKING DELICIOUS. Those shitty spongy cup things the store sells can't even come close to the real deal.

MAKES ENOUGH FOR 8

STRAWBERRY FILLING

1 pound strawberries
2 to 4 tablespoons sugar

SHORTCAKE BISCUITS

1¼ cups whole wheat pastry flour
1 cup white flour
1 tablespoon baking powder
2 tablespoons sugar
½ teaspoon salt
1 cup canned coconut milk
½ teaspoon vanilla extract

Whipped Cream (page 192)*

1 Make the filling: Chop the strawberries up into pieces the size of a button and throw them in a bowl. If your strawberries are super ripe and taste dope as fuck, then add just 2 tablespoons of sugar. Otherwise add the 4 tablespoons and curse your shitty produce. Stir that all together and let it chill while you make everything else.

2 Crank your oven to 425°F. Line a baking sheet with parchment paper.

3 For the biscuits: Sift together the flours, baking powder, sugar, and salt. Make a crater in the middle and add the coconut milk and vanilla. Stir that all together until everything is combined into a shaggy dough. If you need more liquid, add a tablespoon or two of coconut milk to fix that shit.

4 Throw the dough onto a countertop with some flour on it. Pat it into a roughly 8 x 5-inch rectangle about 1½ inches thick. Don't overwork the dough and make it tough. DON'T. Using a biscuit cutter or open end of a glass, cut out all the motherfucking biscuits you can. Aim for 8. Put them on the baking sheet and bake until the bottoms are golden, 12 to 15 minutes. Let them cool for a minute before you go to town.

5 To assemble the shortcakes, cut the biscuits in half like 2 layers of a cake. Layer the strawberry filling on the bottom half, add a scoop of whipped cream, and put the top half of the biscuit back on. Add another layer of strawberries and whipped cream on top and serve right away.

* *Double the whipped cream recipe if you are serving all the biscuits at the same time.*

DON'T SHORTCHANGE DESSERT

SPREAD THE SHORTCAKE
LOVE WITH STRAWBERRIES

WHIPPED CREAM

MAKES ABOUT $1^1/_2$ CUPS

1 can (13.5 ounces) coconut milk, well chilled*

2 tablespoons powdered sugar

½ teaspoon vanilla extract (optional)

* *Put that shit in the fridge the day before so you know it's cold enough. This is not a 30-minute chill kinda situation. You want to give everything time to get cold and for the fat to separate from the coconut water in there. Fuck it—just store a bunch of cans in the fridge so you're always ready.*

1 You need some electric beaters or a stand mixer to do this shit. Stick the bowl and the beaters in the freezer for 15 minutes to let those bastards get chilly.

2 Take them out after 15 minutes and grab the coconut milk from the fridge without shaking it up. Open up the can and scoop out all the thick white cream on the surface and put it in the chilled bowl. Leave that clearish liquid in the can and use it for a smoothie or something later. You don't need that shit now. Sift in the powdered sugar so that there aren't any chunks and add the vanilla.

3 Now beat the fuck out of it on medium-high speed until it starts looking all fluffy and whipped, 1 to 2 minutes. Serve right away. It tastes good for a couple days, but it loses some of its airiness the longer it sits.

BETTER CALL DIBS
ON LICKING THE BEATER
FUCKING QUICK

MAPLE-OAT BANANA BREAD

Forget that banana cake bullshit you're used to eating and telling yourself it's healthy. This is the real fucking deal. A fistful of fiber with just the right amount of sweetness, this loaf will have you coming back for more.

MAKES 1 LOAF

- 2 cups oat flour*
- 1 cup whole wheat pastry flour
- 1¾ teaspoons baking soda
- ¾ teaspoon ground cinnamon
- ½ teaspoon salt
- ¼ cup almond or other nondairy milk
- ¼ teaspoon apple cider vinegar
- 2 cups mashed banana**
- ⅓ cup maple syrup
- 3 tablespoons olive oil
- 1 teaspoon vanilla extract
- 1 tablespoon sugar

1 Heat your oven to 350°F. Grease and flour a standard loaf pan so your bread won't stick. This shit is critical, so DO NOT skip this step.

2 Grab a medium bowl and mix together the flours, baking soda, cinnamon, and salt. Set that aside.

3 In a small glass, mix together the milk and vinegar. Then grab a large bowl and mix together the mashed banana, maple syrup, olive oil, and vanilla. Once all that is mixed up, add the milk mixture and blend that motherfucker all over again. Add the dry ingredients to the wet stuff and mix until there are no more dry spots in the batter.

4 Pour the batter into your loaf pan that you ALREADY GOT READY (RIGHT?) and sprinkle the sugar over the top. This is just for looks because this bread is vain as fuck. Bake it until the top is golden and a toothpick comes out clean when you stab it through your bread, 30 to 40 minutes. When the bread it done, take it out of the loaf pan and let it cool a bit before diving in.

* *This might sound fancy, but just buy cheap rolled oats, throw them in a blender or food processor, and run it until that shit looks like flour. Done.*

** *Don't leave any big chunks or you will have weird uncooked, soggy pockets in your bread. You'll need about 4 bananas to get here.*

CARROT CAKE COOKIES

These cookies are moist and cakey, just like it says in their motherfucking name. They're good for when you have a craving but don't want a whole damn cake to yourself.

MAKES ABOUT 20 COOKIES

- 1½ cups flour (whole wheat pastry or white)
- ½ cup packed light brown sugar
- 1 teaspoon baking powder
- ½ teaspoon salt
- ½ teaspoon ground cinnamon
- ½ teaspoon ground ginger
- 1 cup shredded carrots*
- ½ cup plain almond or other nondairy milk
- ¼ cup olive or grapeseed oil
- ½ cup chopped walnuts
- ½ cup raisins or chopped candied ginger**

1 Heat your oven to 375°F. Line a baking sheet with parchment paper.

2 In a large bowl, mix together the flour, brown sugar, baking powder, salt, cinnamon, and ground ginger. Make sure there are no lumps of brown sugar hanging around in there. In a smaller bowl, mix together the shredded carrots, milk, and oil. Pour the wet ingredients into the dry ones and stir all that shit until there are only a couple dry spots. Fold in the nuts and raisins and stir until there aren't any dry spots.

3 Scoop spoonfuls of the dough onto the baking sheet about 1 inch apart. Bake until the bottoms are golden brown, 18 to 22 minutes. Then do whatever the fuck you do with freshly baked cookies.

* *That's about 2 medium carrots on a box grater.*

** *This shit is optional. These cookies are just as dope without them, too.*

CHOCOLATE CHIP AND ALMOND BUTTER COOKIES

Just like the classic but without all the butter. These chocolatey, nutty masterpieces go pretty damn well with an ice-cold glass of Blended Earl Grey Latte (see page 137 for a photo of both). Go ahead, take a cookie break. You probably did something today to deserve a cookie.

MAKES ABOUT 24 COOKIES

1½ cups whole wheat pastry flour
½ teaspoon baking powder
½ teaspoon baking soda
½ teaspoon salt
⅔ cup chilled almond butter*
⅓ cup brown sugar
⅓ cup white sugar
2 tablespoons ground flaxseed
¾ cup almond milk
1½ teaspoons vanilla extract
½ to ⅔ cup semisweet chocolate chips**

1 In a medium bowl, sift together the flour, baking powder, baking soda, and salt.

2 In the large bowl of a stand mixer or just a big-ass bowl, mix together the almond butter and sugars until it looks kinda creamy and fluffy. Slowly add in the ground flaxseed, almond milk, and vanilla until a loose batter forms in there.

3 When all of that is mixed up, add the sifted flour stuff slowly into the bowl. Mix that up until there are no more dry spots. Fold in the chocolate chips, cover, and put that tasty-ass batter in the fridge for at least 1 hour and for up to 2 days.

4 When you are ready for some cookies, heat your oven to 350°F. Line a baking sheet with parchment paper.

5 Scoop out a spoonful of dough onto the sheet and kind of flatten it out a bit until you get about a 2-inch-wide cookie. Keep going until you fucking run out of dough and then bake until the bottoms are nice and golden, 15 to 18 minutes. Take them off the sheet and let them cool on a wire rack for at least 10 minutes before serving.

* *It really helps the dough come together if this shit is cold, so just stick it in the fridge. You could use peanut butter if that's all you got, but that is a totally different kind of cookie—just know that shit.*

** *Depends on how much chocolate you like in your cookies. That's your fucking call.*

WHO NEEDS A
FUCKING
RADIO
WHEN YOU'VE GOT
SCONES

BLUEBERRY WALNUT LAVENDER SCONES

Scones are the bastard blend of a biscuit and muffin. They sound so wrong but taste so right.

MAKES ABOUT 12 SCONES. BEST SERVED THE DAY THEY ARE MADE.

2¾ cups whole wheat pastry flour
1 tablespoon baking powder
3 tablespoons white sugar, plus more for sprinkling
2 tablespoons brown sugar
¼ teaspoon salt
¼ cup refined coconut oil
2 teaspoons dried lavender*
1¼ cups plain almond milk, plus more for brushing
1 teaspoon vanilla extract
¾ cup fresh or frozen blueberries
½ cup chopped walnuts

1 Crank your oven to 425°F. Line a baking sheet with parchment paper or foil.

2 In a large bowl, mix together the flour, baking powder, sugars, and salt. Cut the oil into the flour using your hands until it all looks kind of grainy and there are no large chunks left. Stir in the motherfucking lavender.

3 Make a well in the center of the flour mixture and pour in the almond milk and vanilla. Mix it together until it is almost all the way combined but stop short. Fold in the berries and walnuts but be careful not to overmix.

4 Scoop out the dough in ½-cup measurements and plop onto the baking sheet. Brush with almond milk and sprinkle with white sugar. Bake until they look a little golden around on the bottom, 12 to 15 minutes.

* *Can't find dried lavender? Don't trek all over town. Just leave it out and add an extra ½ teaspoon vanilla extract. We just wanted to give you a chance to be extra fancy.*

SHREDDED CARROT AND APPLE MUFFINS

With 2 servings of produce packed in this grab-and-go breakfast, these muffins mean fucking business.

MAKES 12 STANDARD MUFFINS

- 2¼ cups whole wheat pastry flour
- ½ cup sugar
- 1 tablespoon baking powder
- 1½ teaspoons ground cinnamon
- ½ teaspoon salt
- 1¼ cups almond or other nondairy milk
- 1½ cups grated carrots*
- ⅓ cup grated apple**
- ¼ cup olive or grapeseed oil
- 1 tablespoon lemon juice
- 1 teaspoon vanilla extract
- ½ cup chopped nuts like walnuts or almonds (optional as fuck)

1 Heat your oven to 375°F. Grab a muffin tin and grease that fucker up or throw in some muffin liners.

2 In a big bowl, whisk together the flour, sugar, baking powder, cinnamon, and salt. In a smaller bowl, stir together the almond milk, carrots, apple, oil, lemon juice, and vanilla until everything is pretty well combined. See any big-ass globs of carrots? Keep stirring.

3 Pour the wet ingredients into the flour mixture and stir until just combined. If you mix it up too much, your muffins will be tough and sad. Don't fuck this up after you did all that grating. Fold in the nuts now if you are using them.

4 Scoop the batter into the muffin cups and bake until a toothpick comes out clean when poked in the center of a muffin, 18 to 20 minutes. Take them out of the tin to cool for at least 15 minutes before eating.

* *About 3 medium carrots*

** *About 1 small apple. Just use whatever kind you would normally eat.*

PEANUT BUTTER AND BANANA NUT MUFFINS

This is the Elvis of muffins. So bow the fuck down to the king and his great taste.

MAKES 12 STANDARD MUFFINS

2 cups whole wheat pastry or all-purpose flour
1 tablespoon baking powder
½ teaspoon salt
½ cup creamy peanut butter
½ cup packed light brown sugar
¾ cup plain almond or other nondairy milk
1½ cups mashed ripe banana*
1 teaspoon vanilla extract
½ cup chopped walnuts or peanuts**

1 Heat your oven to 375°F. Grab your muffin tin and grease that bastard or use paper muffin liners.

2 In a big bowl, mix together the flour, baking powder, and salt. Set the fucker aside.

3 Now in a smaller bowl, mix together the peanut butter and brown sugar until it looks kinda creamy. Stir in the milk, banana, and vanilla until everything is mixed up.

4 Pour the wet ingredients into the dry and stir until just combined. If you mix it up too much, your muffins will be tough. Don't waste all that peanut butter on some fucked-up muffins. Fold in the nuts now if you are using them.

5 Scoop the batter into the muffin cups. This makes a lot of batter, so fill those fuckers to the brim so you get nice, domed, bakery-style muffins. Bake until a toothpick comes out clean when poked in the center of a muffin, 18 to 22 minutes. Take them out of the tin and let cool for at least 15 minutes before eating.

* *This usually takes about 3 regular-size bananas.*

** *You could sub ½ cup chocolate chips in here if you want to drop any illusions that these fuckers aren't dessert.*

COCONUT CORNMEAL CAKE

This sweet, buttery dessert is the perfect marriage between cornbread and yellow cake. It's so fucking right it hurts. Keep it simple and top it with fresh fruit and a little Whipped Cream (page 192). Save frosting for something that needs the help.

ENOUGH FOR 8 PEOPLE

- **$1\frac{1}{4}$ cups cornmeal***
- **$\frac{3}{4}$ cup whole wheat pastry flour or white flour**
- **$\frac{3}{4}$ cup sugar**
- **2 teaspoons baking powder**
- **$\frac{1}{2}$ teaspoon salt**
- **$1\frac{1}{2}$ cups canned coconut milk**
- **1 teaspoon vanilla extract**
- **$\frac{1}{2}$ teaspoon grated lemon zest**

1 First, heat your oven to 375°F. Grab an 8-inch cake pan, grease it, and dust it with flour to make sure your cake doesn't stick. If you are still consumed with fear, cut a round out of parchment paper the same size as the pan and stick that in the bottom to be extra fucking sure your cake will come out in one piece. Now relax, you got this shit.

2 Get a big bowl and whisk together the cornmeal, flour, sugar, baking powder, and salt. Make a crater in the center of the dry mixture and pour in the coconut milk, vanilla, and lemon zest and stir it all up until there are no dry pockets and very few lumps.

3 Pour that batter into your cake pan that you prepped earlier because you followed the goddamn directions. Let somebody else lick the spoon and the bowl because 1) The batter is tasty as hell and 2) They will now owe you one. Cash in that favor the next time you need help moving. You're fucking welcome.

4 Bake the cake until a toothpick stuck in the center comes out clean, 30 to 40 minutes. Let it cool in the pan for 15 minutes and then turn it out on to a wire rack to finish cooling until you're ready for it.

5 Serve cold or at room temperature.

* *The finely ground stuff you would use to make cornbread, not that coarser shit you would use to make polenta. Got it?*

MORE
CAKE STANDS
LESS
KEG STANDS

BANANA CREAM PIE

This may not look like the fanciest pie, but it's the only one that ALWAYS hits the fucking sweet spot.

MAKES 1 PIE, ENOUGH FOR 8 PEOPLE

PRESS-IN CRUST

1½ cups flour*
1 tablespoon sugar
½ teaspoon salt
¼ teaspoon baking powder
¼ cup refined coconut oil**
2 tablespoons olive or grapeseed oil
2 to 3 tablespoons almond milk

VANILLA CUSTARD FILLING

¼ cup cornstarch or arrowroot powder
¼ cup sugar
Pinch of salt
1 can (13.5 ounces) coconut milk
1 cup plain almond or other nondairy milk
1½ teaspoons vanilla extract

3 large ripe bananas
Whipped Cream (page 192)

1 Make the crust: Heat your oven to 350°F. Grab a standard pie plate.

2 In a medium bowl, mix together the flour, sugar, salt, and baking powder. Crumble the coconut oil into the flour using your fingers and break up pieces bigger than a pea. It should look kinda like coarse sand from a shitty playground. You can throw this all in your food processor too, just run it until you get the same texture, and then put it in a bowl.

3 Pour in the olive oil and 2 tablespoons of the almond milk and stir it all up with a fork until a shaggy dough comes together. If it still looks dry, add the remaining tablespoon of milk. Press the dough into the pie plate so that it's even and going up the sides. You know how a pie crust should look. (At this point, you can stick that shit in the fridge to bake later or get right down to business. Your call.)

4 Line the inside of your crust with foil and pour a bunch of dried beans in there that you aren't planning on eating. This weird shit keeps the crust in place while it bakes. Trust the system. Throw this in the oven for 12 minutes, then pull it out and remove the foil and beans. Stick it back in the oven until the bottom looks cooked and the edges are golden, another 12 to 15 minutes. Let it cool while you make the filling.

5 Make the custard filling: In a medium saucepan, whisk together the cornstarch, sugar, and salt. Slowly whisk in around ⅓ cup of the coconut milk, making sure there aren't any clumps. Once all the starch is dissolved, whisk in the remaining coconut milk, the almond milk, and vanilla.

* *You can use whole wheat pastry, all-purpose, or a combo here. All of it will work.*

** *You don't want the oil all runny and melted. It should look milky and have a consistency similar to room temp butter. If it's hot in your place, stick that shit in the fridge for a minute or two to cool down.*

6 Put the pot over medium-high heat and keep whisking until the mixture is bubbling and you can feel it start to thicken to sort of a gravy texture, about 5 minutes. Now, turn down the heat to medium-low and grab a spatula. Keep the pot at a very gentle simmer and keep scraping the bottom and sides with a spatula to avoid pudding skin. That shit is gross. Keep this up for 7 to 10 minutes or until you flick some of the custard across the top of itself in the pot and that spot holds its shape for a couple seconds. Gross but fucking accurate.

7 Your pie crust should be cool enough to handle now. Slice up the bananas into rounds no thicker than ½ inch. Line the crust with the banana slices, like all over the fucking place. Up the sides, BANANAS EVERYWHERE. Now pour the warm custard into the banana-lined pie shell. Cover and place this fucker in the fridge for at least 3 hours.

8 Once the custard has cooled and set, spread on a batch of the whipped cream over the top and serve. This pie is best eaten within 3 days of being made because the bananas cannot be trusted to keep their shit together much longer than that.

DINNER ON THE FLOOR
CALL THAT MESSGHETTI

thanks

MD: Thanks to my family who didn't take me to the clinic when I told them I went viral; to VJ and Rebecca who are always willing to throw down in the kitchen; to Nick who goes big at every fucking buffet and with every new recipe; to Mike for having my back from the jump; to Seth and Amber who are always telling me to dream bigger; to Alex for all of her faith; and to Jade, who I know appreciates a good come-up story. Thanks also to all the motherfuckers I worked with at the grocery stores in San Diego and LA. You guys tried all my food, made me laugh, and kept me from losing my fucking mind. I would have burned it all down without you. And last, but not least, the Internet. You did this, I just helped.

MH: Thanks to my family for all the meals we've shared no matter how good, bad, or ugly; to Baltasar for being as supportive as he was understanding of my second job; to DeVoll for teaching me education doesn't stop when school ends; to Jen for always wanting to take a break and chat about food; to Brian and Patrick for the late-night laughs; to Amir and Channing for all that soul-searching shit; to the Harrisons for always letting me stay for dinner; and to the baddest bitch I know, Phoenix, for the infinite inspiration. Y'all have kept me smiling and sane through everything. And to the Internet, truly the greatest thing since sliced bread. This would not have been possible without the love and support of a bunch of strangers.

And of course none of this would be possible without the gang at Rodale—Alex, Kara, Mary Ann, Kristin, Yelena, Aly, Brent, and Nancy; Lauren, Richard, and Kim at Inkwell; and Sally at Stroock. Also Scott Horne, Richard Villalobos, and Mr. Nick Wagner. Thanks for throwing your love and support behind a couple of randos with a blog.

Underscored page references indicate sidebars. **Boldface** references indicate photographs. Fucking details.

C

L

M

N

S

T

U

V

W

Y

Z